HANDBOOK OF NATURE STUDY:

BIRDS

COMPLETE YOUR COLLECTION TODAY!

Handbook of Nature-Study:

Birds

ANNA BOTSFORD COMSTOCK, B.S., L.H.D

LATE PROFESSOR OF NATURE-STUDY IN CORNELL UNIVERSITY

LIVING BOOK
PRESS

This edition published 2020
by Living Book Press

ISBN: 978-1-922348-46-3 (hardcover)
         978-1-922348-47-0 (softcover)

A catalogue record for this book is available from the National Library of Australia

CONTENTS

BIRDS

BIRDS

A loggerhead shrike adult feeding some recent fledglings

BIRDS

THE reason for studying any bird is to ascertain what it does; in order to accomplish this, it is necessary to know what the bird is, learning what it is, being simply a step that leads to a knowledge of what it does. But, to hear some of our bird devotees talk, one would think that to be able to identify a bird is all of bird study. On the contrary, the identification of birds is simply the alphabet to the real study, the alphabet by means of which we may spell out the life habits of the bird. To know these habits is the ambition of the true ornithologist, and should likewise be the ambition of the beginner, even though the beginner be a young child.

Several of the most common birds have been selected as subjects for lessons in this book; other common birds, like the phoebe and wrens, have been omitted purposely; after the children have studied the birds, as indicated in the lessons, they will enjoy working out lessons for themselves with other birds. Naturally, the sequence of these lessons does not follow scientific classification; in the first ten lessons, an attempt has been made to lead the child gradually into a knowledge of bird life. Beginning with the chicken there follow naturally the lessons with pigeons and the canary; then there follows the careful and detailed study of the robins and constant comparison of them with the blue birds. This is enough for the first year in the primary grades. The next year the work begins with the birds that remain in the North during the winter, the chickadee, nuthatch and downy

These 20 day old barn swallows are starting to take small test flights but are still being fed in the nest.

woodpecker. After these have been studied carefully, the teacher may be an opportunist when spring comes and select any of the lessons when the bird subjects are at hand. The classification suggested for the woodpeckers and the swallows is for more advanced pupils, as are the lessons on the geese and turkeys. It is to be hoped that these lessons will lead the child directly to the use of the bird manuals, of which there are several excellent ones.

BEGINNING BIRD STUDY IN THE PRIMARY GRADES

The hen is especially adapted as an object lesson for the young beginner of bird study. First of all, she is a bird, notwithstanding the adverse opinions of two of my small pupils who stoutly maintained that "a robin is a bird, but a hen is a hen." Moreover, the hen is a bird always available for nature-study; she looks askance at us from the crates of the world's marts; she comes to meet us in the country barnyard, stepping toward us sedately; looking at us earnestly, with one eye, then turning her head so as to check up her observations with the other; meantime she asks us a little question in a wheedling, soft tone, which we understand perfectly to mean "have you perchance brought me something to eat?" Not only is the hen an interesting bird in her-

A commong blackbird (Turdus merula) *on her nest.*

self, but she is a bird with problems; and by studying her carefully we may be introduced into the very heart and center of bird life.

This lesson may be presented in two ways: First, if the pupils live in the country where they have poultry at home, the whole series of lessons may best be accomplished through interested talks on the part of the teacher, which should be followed on the part of the children, by observations, which should be made at home and the results given in school in oral or written lessons. Second, if the pupils are not familiar with fowls, a hen and a chick, if possible, should be kept in a cage in the schoolroom for a few days, and a duck or gosling should be brought in one day for observation. The crates in which fowls are sent to market make very good cages. One of the teachers of the Elmira, N. Y. Schools introduced into the basement of the schoolhouse a hen, which there hatched her brood of chicks, much to the children's delight and edification. After the pupils have become thoroughly interested in the hen and are familiar with her ways, after they have fed her and watched her, and have for her a sense of ownership, the following lessons may be given in an informal manner, as if they were naturally suggested to the teacher's mind through watching the fowl.

Feathers as Clothing

THE bird's clothing affords a natural beginning for bird study because the wearing of feathers is a most striking character distinguishing birds from other creatures; also, feathers and flying are the first things the young child notices about birds.

The purpose of all of these lessons on the hen are: (a) To induce the child to make continued and sympathetic observations on the habits of the domestic birds. (b) To cause him involuntarily to compare the domestic with the wild birds. (c) To induce him to think for himself why the shape of the body, wings, head, beak, feet, legs and feathers are adapted in each species to protect the bird and assist it in getting its living.

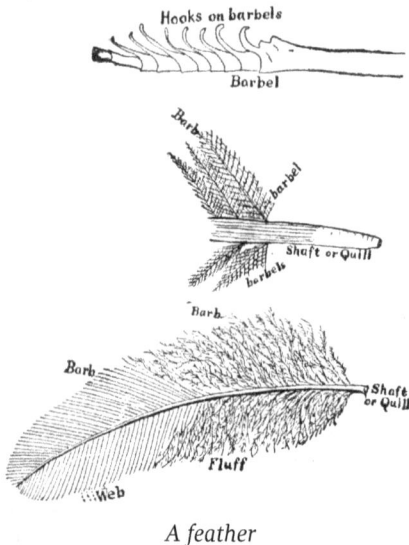

A feather

The overlapping of the feathers on a hen's back and breast is a pretty illustration of nature's method of shingling, so that the rain, finding no place to enter, drips off, leaving the bird's underclothing quite dry. It is interesting to note how a hen behaves in the rain; she droops her tail and holds herself so that the water finds upon her no resting place, but simply a steep surface down which to flow to the ground.

Each feather consists of three parts, the shaft or quill, which is the central stiff stem of the feather, giving it strength. From this quill come off the barbs which, toward the outer end, join together in a smooth web, making the thin, fan-like portion of the feather; at the base is the fluff, which is soft and downy and near to the body of the fowl. The teacher should put on the blackboard this figure so that incidentally the pupils may learn the parts of a feather and their struc-

Feathers help birds to endure the cold.

ture. If a microscope is available, show both the web and the fluff of a feather under a three-fourths objective.

The feathers on the back of a hen are longer and narrower in proportion than those on the breast and are especially fitted to protect the back from rain; the breast feathers are shorter and have more of the fluff, thus protecting the breast from the cold as well as the rain. It is plain to any child that the soft fluff is comparable to our woolen underclothing while the smooth, overlapping web forms a rain and wind-proof outer coat. Down is a feather with no quill; young chicks are covered with down. A pin-feather is simply a young feather rolled up in a sheath, which bursts later and is shed, leaving the feather free to assume its form. Take a large pin-feather and cut the sheath open and show the pupils the young feather lying within.

When a hen oils her feathers it is a process well worth observing. The oil gland is on her back just at the base of the tail feathers; she squeezes the gland with her beak to get the oil and then rubs the beak over the surface of her feathers and passes them through it; she spends more time oiling the feathers on her back and breast than those on the other parts, so that they will surely shed water. Country people say when the hen oils her feathers, it is a sure sign of rain. The hen sheds her feathers once a year and is a most untidy looking bird meanwhile, a fact that she seems to realize, and is as shy and cross as a young lady caught in company in curl papers; but she seems very pleased with herself when she finally gains her new feathers.

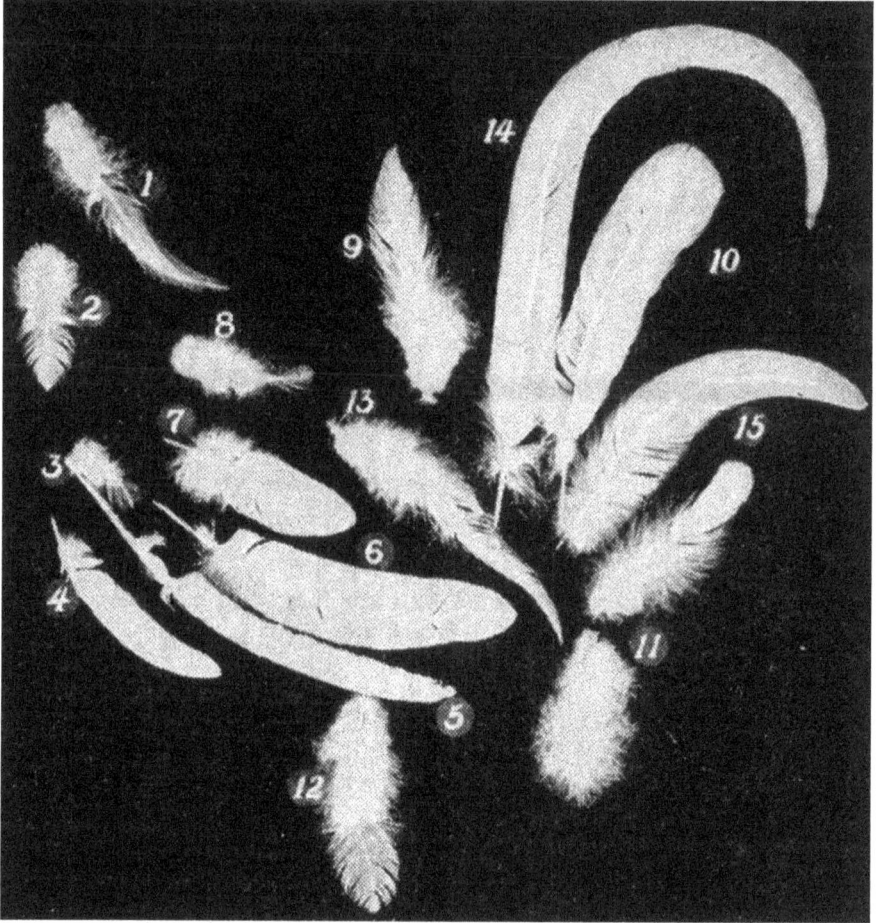

Feathers of a rooster, showing their relative size, shape and position.

1. neck hackle; 2. breast; 3. wing shoulder covert; 4. wing flight covert; 5. wing primary; 6. wing secondary; 7. wing covert; 8. back; 9. tail covert; 10. main tail; 11. fluff; 12. thigh; 13. saddle hackle; 14. the sickle or feather of beauty; 15. lesser sickle.

Leading thought— Feathers grow from the skin of a bird and protect the bird from rain, snow, wind and cold. Some of the feathers act as cloaks or mackintoshes and others as underclothing.

Method— The hen should be at close range for this lesson where the children may observe how and where the different kinds of feathers grow. The pupils should also study separately the form of a feather from the back, from the breast, from the under side of the body, and a pin-feather.

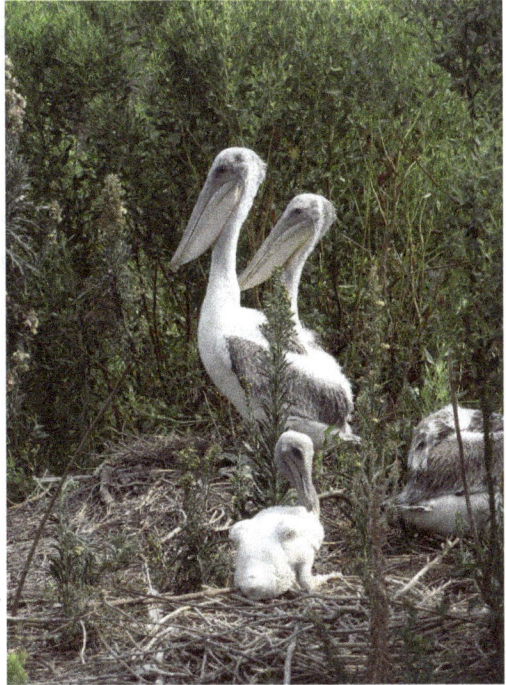

Pelicans are born naked, but are soon covered with white down.

Observations—

1. How are the feathers arranged on the back of the hen? Are they like shingles on the roof? If so, what for?

2. How does a hen look when standing in the rain?

3. How are the feathers arranged on the breast?

4. Compare a feather from the back and one from the breast and note the difference.

5. Are both ends of these feathers alike? If not, what is the difference?

6. Is the fluffy part of the feather on the outside or next to the bird's skin? What is its use?

7. Why is the smooth part of the feather (the web) on the outside?

8. Some feathers are all fluff and are called "down." At what age was the fowl all covered with down?

9. What is a pin-feather? What makes you think so?

10. How do hens keep their feathers oily and glossy so they will shed water?

11. Where does the hen get the oil? Describe how she oils her feathers and which ones does she oil most? Does she oil her feathers before a rain?

> *"How beautiful your feathers be!"*
> *The Redbird sang to the Tulip-tree*
> *New garbed in autumn gold.*
> *"Alas!" the bending branches sighed,*
> *"They cannot like your leaves abide*
> *To keep us from the cold!"*
>
> —John B. Tabb.

Not a candidate for a beauty contest...
Look at the pin feathers!

Feathers as Ornament

TEACHER'S STORY

THE ornamental plumage of birds is one of the principal illustrations of a great principle of evolution. The theory is that the male birds win their mates because of their beauty, those that are not beautiful being doomed to live single and leave no progeny to inherit their dullness. On the other hand, the successful wooer hands down his beauty to his sons. However, another quite different principle acts upon the coloring of the plumage of the mother birds; for if they should develop bright colors themselves, they would attract the eyes of the enemy to their precious hidden nests; only by being inconspicuous, are they able to protect their eggs and nestlings from discovery and death. The mother partridge, for instance, is so nearly the color of the dead leaves

Peacock feathers. Is beauty useful?

on the ground about her, that we may almost step upon her before we discover her; if she were the color of the oriole or tanager she would very soon be the center of attraction to every prowler. Thus, it has come about that among the birds the feminine love of beauty has developed the gorgeous colors of the males, while the need for protection of the home has kept the female plumage modest and unnoticeable.

The curved feathers of the rooster's tail are weak and mobile and could not possibly be of any use as a rudder; but they give grace and beauty to the fowl and cover the useful rudder feathers underneath by a feather fountain of iridescence. The neck plumage of the cock is also often luxurious and beautiful in color and quite different from that of the hen. Among the ducks the brilliant blue-green iridescent head of the drake and his wing bars are beautiful, and make his wife seem Quaker-like in contrast.

As an object lesson to instil the idea that the male bird is proud of his beautiful feathers, I know of none better than that presented by the turkey gobbler, for he is a living expression of self-conscious

A peacock showing off its colors

vanity. He spreads his tail to the fullest extent and shifts it this way and that to show the exquisite play of colors over the feathers in the sunlight, meanwhile throwing out his chest to call particular attention to his blue and red wattles; and to keep from bursting with pride he bubbles over in vainglorious "gobbles."

The hen with her chicks and the turkey hen with her brood, if they follow their own natures, must wander in the fields for food. If they were bright in color, the hawks would soon detect them and their chances of escape would be small; this is another instance of the advantage to the young of adopting the colors of the mother rather than of the father; a fact equally true of the song birds in cases where the males are brilliant in color at maturity. The Baltimore oriole does not assist his mate in brooding, but he sits somewhere on the home tree and cheers her by his glorious song and by glimpses of his gleaming orange coat. Some have accused him of being lazy; on the contrary, he is a wise householder for, instead of attracting the attention of crow or squirrel to his nest, he distracts their attention from it by both color and song.

A peacock's feather should really be a lesson by itself, it is so much a thing of beauty. The brilliant color of the purple eye-spot, and the graceful flowing barbs that form the setting to the central gem, are all a training in aesthetics as well as in nature-study. After the children have studied such a feather let them see the peacock either in reality or in picture and give them stories about this bird of Juno; a bird so inconspicuous if it were not for his great spread of tail, that a child seeing it first cried, "Oh, oh, see this old hen all in bloom!"

The whole question of sexual selection may be made as plain as need be for the little folks, by simply telling them that the mother bird chooses for her mate the one which is most brightly and beautifully dressed, and make much of the comb and wattles of the rooster and gobbler as additions to the brilliancy of their appearance.

LESSON

Leading thought— The color of feathers and often their shape are for the purpose of making birds more beautiful; while in others, the color of the feathers protects them from the observation of their enemies.

Methods— While parts of this lesson relating to fowls, may be given in primary grades, it is equally fitted for pupils who have a wider knowledge of birds. Begin with a comparison of the plumage of the hen and the rooster. Then, if possible, study the turkey gobbler and a peacock in life or in pictures. Also the plumage of a Rouen duck and drake, and if possible, the Baltimore oriole, the goldfinch, the scarlet tanager and the cardinal.

Observations—

1. Note difference in shape and color of the tail feathers of hen and rooster.

2. Do the graceful curved tail feathers of the rooster help him in flying? Are they stiff enough to act as a rudder?

3. If not of use in flying what are they for? Which do you think the more beautiful: the hen or the rooster?

4. In what respects is the rooster a more beautiful fowl?

5. What other parts of the rooster's plumage is more beautiful than that of the hen?

6. If a turkey gobbler sees you looking at him he begins to strut. Do you think he does this to show off his tail feathers? Note how he turns his spread tail this way and that so the sunshine will bring out

the beautiful changeable colors. Do you think he does this so you can see and admire him?

7. Describe the difference in plumage between the hen turkey and the gobbler. Does the hen turkey strut?

8. Note the beautiful blue-green iridescent head and wing patches on the wings of the Rouen ducks. Is the drake more beautiful than the duck?

9. What advantage is it for these fowls to have the father bird more beautiful and bright in color than the mother bird?

10. In case of the Baltimore oriole is the mother bird as bright in color as the father bird? Why?

11. Study a peacock's feather. What color is the eye-spot? What color around that? What color and shape are the outside barbs of the feather? Do you blame a peacock for being proud when he can spread a tail of a hundred eyes? Does the peahen have such beautiful tail feathers as the peacock?

The bird of Juno glories in his plumes;
Pride makes the fowl to preene his feathers so.
His spotted train fetched from old Argus' head,
With golden rays like to the brightest sun,
Inserteth self-love in the silly bird;
Till midst its hot and glorious fumes
He spies his feet and then lets fall his plumes.
—"THE PEACOCK", ROBERT GREENE (1560).

Common tern. While we are having winter this bird spends the summer in South America. It will return to spend our summer with us

How Birds Fly

TEACHER'S STORY

TO convince the children that a bird's wings correspond to our arms, they should see a fowl with its feathers off, prepared for market or oven, and they will infer the fact at once.

The bird flies by lifting itself through pressing down upon the air with its wings. There are several experiments which are needed to make the child understand this. It is difficult for children to conceive that the air is really anything, because they cannot see it; so the first experiment should be to show that the air is something we can push against or that pushes against us. Strike the air with a fan and we feel there is something which the fan pushes; we feel the wind when it is blowing and it is very difficult for us to walk against a hard wind. If we hold an open umbrella in the hand while we jump from a step we feel buoyed up because the umbrella presses down upon the air. The bird presses down upon the air with the wings, just as the open umbrella does. The bird flies by pressing down upon the air with its wings just as a boy jumps high by pressing down with his hands on his vaulting pole.

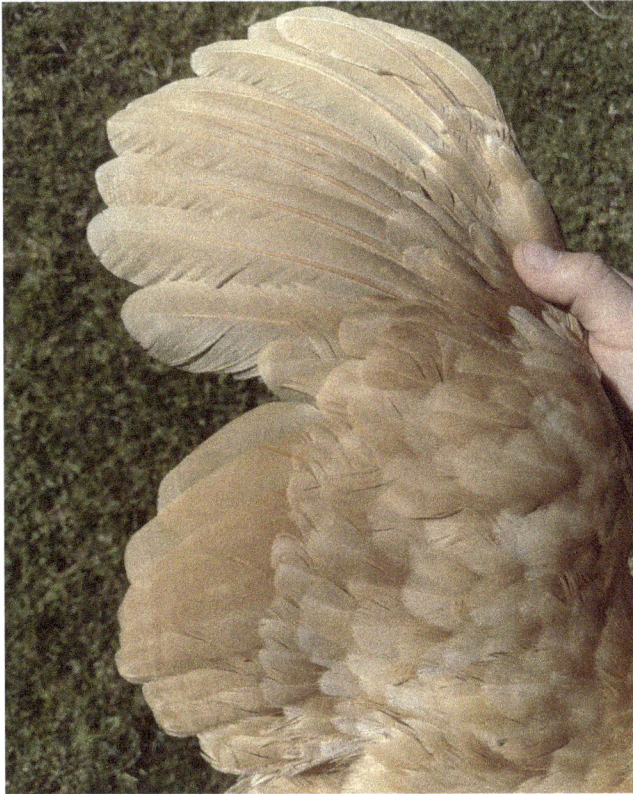

A hens wing outstretched showing primaries and secondaries of the wing and the overlapping of the feathers.

Study wing and note: (a) That the wings open and close at the will of the bird. (b) That the feathers open and shut on each other like a fan. (c) When the wing is open the wing quills overlap, so that the air cannot pass through them. (d) When the wing is open it is curved so that it is more efficient, for the same reason that an umbrella presses harder against the atmosphere when it is open than when it is broken by the wind and turned wrong side out.

A wing feather has the barbs on the front edge lying almost parallel to the quill while those on the hind edge come off at a wide angle. The reason for this is easy to see, for this feather has to cut the air as the bird flies; and if the barbs on the front side were like those of the other side they would be torn apart by the wind. The barbs on the hind side of the feather form a strong, close web so as to press down on the air and not let it through. The wing quill is curved; the convex side is up and the concave side below during flight. The concave side, like the umbrella, catches more air than the upper side; the down stroke of the wing is forward and down; while on the up stroke, as the wing is lifted, it bends at the joint like a fan turned sidewise, and offers less surface to resist the air. Thus, the up stroke does not push the bird down.

Observations should be made on the use of the bird's tail in flight. The hen spreads her tail like a fan when she flies to the top of the fence; the robin does likewise when in flight. The fact that the tail is used as a rudder to guide the bird in flight, as well as to give more surface for pressing down upon the air, is hard for the younger pupils to understand, and perhaps can be best taught by watching the erratic unbalanced flight of young birds whose tail feathers are not yet grown.

The tail feather differs from the wing feather in that the quill is not curved, and the barbs on each side are of about equal length and lie at about the same angle on each side the quill.

References— The Bird Book, Eckstorm, pp. 75-92; Story of the Birds, Baskett, pp. 171-176; Bird Life, Chapman, p. 18; The Bird, Beebe, Ch. XIII; First Book of Birds, Miller.

LESSON

Leading thought— A bird flies by pressing down upon the air with its wings, which are made especially for this purpose. The bird's tail acts as a rudder during flight.

Method— The hen, it is hoped, will by this time be tame enough so that the teacher may spread open her wings for the children to see. In addition, have a detached wing of a fowl such as are used in farm houses instead of a whisk-broom.

Observations—

1. Do you think a bird's wings correspond to our arms? If so why?

2. Why do birds flap their wings when they start to fly?

3. Can you press against the air with a fan?

4. Why do you jump so high with a vaulting pole? Do you think the bird uses the air as you use the pole?

5. How are the feathers arranged on the wing so that the bird can use it to press down on the air?

6. If you carry an umbrella on a windy morning, which catches more wind, the under or the top side? Why is this? Does the curved surface of the wing act in the same way?

7. Take a wing feather. Are the barbs as long on one side of the quill as on the other? Do they lie at the same angle from the quill on both sides? If not why?

8. Which side of the quill lies on the outer side and which on the inner side of the wing?

9. Is the quill of the feather curved?

10. Which side is uppermost in the wing, the convex or the concave side? Take a quill in one hand and press the tip against the other. Which way does it bend easiest, toward the convex or the concave side? What has this to do with the flight of the bird?

11. If the bird flies by pressing the wings against the air on the down stroke, why does it not push itself downward with its wings on the up stroke?

12. What is the shape and arrangement of the feathers so as to avoid pushing the bird back to earth when it lifts its wings?

13. Why do you have a rudder to a boat?

14. Do you think a bird could sail through the air without something to steer with? What is the bird's rudder?

15. Have you ever seen a young bird whose tail is not yet grown, try to fly? If so, how did it act?

16. Does the hen when she flies keep the tail closed or open like a fan?

17. Compare a tail feather with a wing feather and describe the difference.

Migration of Birds

The travelogues of birds are as fascinating as our favorite stories of fairies, ad venture, and fiction. If we could accompany certain birds, such as the Arctic terns, on their spring and autumn trips, the logs of the trips would be far more ex citing than some recorded by famous aviators. The Arctic tern seems to hold the record for long-distance flight. Its nest is made within the bounds of the Arctic circle and its winter home is in the region of the Antarctic circle. The round-trip mile age for this bird during a year is about 22,000 miles. Wells W. Cooke, a pioneer student of bird migration, has called attention to the interesting fact that the Arctic tern "has more hours of daylight than any other animal on the globe. At the northern nesting-site the midnight sun has already appeared before the birds' arrival, and it never sets during their entire stay at the breeding grounds. During two months of their sojourn in the Antarctic the birds do not see a sunset, and for the rest of the time the sun dips only a little way below the horizon and broad day light is continuous. The birds, therefore, have twenty-four hours of daylight for at least eight months in the year, and during the other four months have considerably more daylight than darkness." It is true that few of our birds take such long trips as does the Arctic tern; but most birds do travel for some distance each spring and fall.

The migration routes of the golden plover. The dotted area is the summer home and nesting place ; the black area is the winter home. Migration routes are indicated by arrows. On the southern route the plover makes a flight of 2,400 miles from Labrador to South America

Each season brings to our attention certain changes in the bird population. During late summer, we see great flocks of swallows; they are on telephone or telegraph wires, wire fences, clothes lines, or aerial wires. They twitter and flutter and seem all excited. For a few days, as they prepare for their southern journey, they are seen in such groups, and then are seen no more until the following spring. Some birds do not gather in flocks before leaving for the winter; they just disappear: and we scarcely know when they go. We may hear their call notes far over our heads as they wing their way to their winter homes. Some birds migrate only during the day, others go only during the night, and others may travel by either day or night. Those birds that do not migrate are called permanent residents. In the United States chickadees, jays, downy woodpeckers, nuthatches, grouse, and pheasants are typical examples of the permanent resident group. These birds must be able to secure food under even the most adverse conditions. Much of their food is insect life found in or about trees; some fruits and buds of trees, shrubs, and vines are also included in their diet.

Birds that travel are called migratory birds. If the spring migrants remain with us for the summer, we call them our summer residents. Fall migrants that remain with us for the winter are called winter residents. The migrants that do not remain with us but pass on to spend the summer or winter in some other area are called our transients or visitors. Of course, we must remember that the birds which visit us only for a short time are summer residents and winter residents in other parts of the country. Our summer residents are the winter residents of some other area.

In spring we await with interest the arrival of the first migrants. These birds are, in general, those which have spent the winter only a comparatively short distance away. In the eastern United States, we expect robins, red-winged blackbirds, song sparrows, and bluebirds among the earliest migrants. In many species the males arrive first; they may come as much as two weeks ahead of the females. The immature birds are usually the last to arrive. The time of arrival of the first migrants is determined somewhat by weather conditions; their dates cannot be predicted with as much accuracy as can those of birds

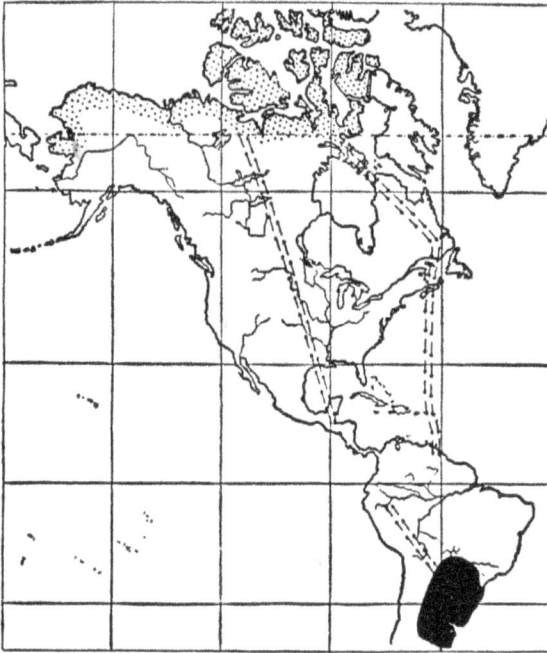

The travels of the bobolink. The migration routes of the bobolink are shorter than those of the plover and follow land more closely

which, having spent the winter at a greater distance from us, arrive later when the weather is more favorable. In some places, for example at Ithaca, New York, bird records have been kept each season for more than thirty years. With the information from these records, it is possible to indicate almost to a day when certain birds, such as barn swallows, orioles, or hummingbirds, may be expected to arrive. Usually the very first birds of a kind to arrive are those individuals which will within a few days continue their northward journey. The later arrivals are usually those that remain to become residents. In some species all individuals are migrants; for southern New York the white-throated sparrow is representative of such a group. It winters far the south and nests farther north than southern New York.

Why do birds migrate? This question has often been asked; but in answer to it we must say that while we know much about where birds go and how fast they travel, we still know actually very little about the reasons for their regular seasonal journeys.

As the airplane pilot has man-made in instruments to aid him in reaching a certain airport, so the birds have a well-developed sense of direction which guides them to their destination. Each kind of bird seems, in general, to take the route followed by its ancestors; but this route may be varied if for any reason food should become scarce along the way. Such routes are so exactly followed year after year that they are known as lanes of migration. Persons desiring to study a certain species of bird can have excellent opportunities to do so by being at some good vantage point along this lane. Some times undue advantage has been taken of certain birds, especially hawks. Persons desiring to kill these birds have collected at strategic points along the lanes and wantonly killed many of them. As a result of such activities sanctuaries have been established at certain places along the lanes to give added protection to birds. The routes north and south followed by a given species of bird may lead over entirely different parts of the country; these are called double migration routes. They may vary so much that one route may lead chiefly over land while the other may lead over the ocean. The golden plover is an example of such a case. See the migration map.

Much valuable information as well as pleasure can be gained from keeping a calendar of migration and other activities of birds. It is especially interesting during the spring months when first arrivals are recorded if daily lists are made of all species observed. In summer, nesting activities and special studies of an individual species provide something of interest for each day. More pleasure can be derived from the hobby if several people take it up and compare their findings. Interests in photography, sketching, of nature-story writing are natural companions of such bird study.

SUGGESTED READING – *Bird Friends*, by - Gilbert H. Trafton; *Bird Life*, by Frank M. Chapman; *Birds and Their Attributes*, by Glover M. Allen; *Birds of America*, edited by T. Gilbert Pearson; *Birds of New York*, by E. H. Eaton; *The Book of Bird Life*, by A. A. Allen; *The Book of Birds*, edited by Gilbert Grosvenor and Alexander Wetmore; *The Children's Book of Birds* (First Book of Birds and Second Book of Birds), by Olive Thorne Miller; *Flight Speed of Birds*, by May Thacher Cooke (U. S. Department of Agriculture, Circular 428); *The Migration of North American Birds*, by Frederick C. Lincoln (U. S. Department of Agriculture, Circular 363); *Nature—by Seaside and Wayside*, by Mary G. Phillips and Julia M. Wright, Book 3, *Plants and Animals; Our Winter Birds*, by Frank M. Chapman; *Pathways in Science*, by Gerald S. Craig and Co-authors, Book 2, *Out-of-doors*, Book 5, *Learning about Our World; The Stir of Nature*, by William H. Carr; *Traveling with the Birds*, by Rudyerd Boulton; *The Travels of Birds*, by Frank M. Chapman.

A Saker Falcon. Notice the strong hooked beak, the keen eye, and the prominent nostril.

Eyes and Ears of Birds

TEACHER'S STORY

THE hen's eyes are placed at the side of the head so that she cannot see the same object with both eyes at the same time, and thus she has the habit of looking at us first with one eye and then the other to be sure she sees correctly; also the position of the hen's eyes give her a command of her entire environment. All birds have much keener eyes than have we; and they can adjust their eyes for either near or far vision much more effectively than we can; the hawk, flying high in the air, can see the mouse on the ground.

There is a wide range of colors found in the eyes of birds; white, red, blue, yellow, brown, gray, pink, purple and green are found in the iris of different species. The hen's eye consists of a black pupil at the center, which must always be black in any eye, since it is a hole through which enters the image of the object. The iris of the hen's eye is yellow; there is apparently no upper lid but the lower lid comes up during the process of sleeping. When the bird is drowsy the little film lid comes out from the corner of the eye and spreads over it like a veil; just at the corner of our own eye, next the nose, is the remains of this film lid, although we cannot move it as the hen does.

The hearing of birds is very acute, although the ear is simply a hole in the side of the head in most cases, and is more or less covered with feathers. The hen's ear is like this in many varieties; but in others and in the roosters there are ornamental ear lobes.

LESSON

Leading thought— The eyes and ears of birds are peculiar and very efficient.

Methods— The hen or chicken and the rooster should be observed for this lesson; notes may be made in the poultry yard or in the school-room when the birds are brought there for study.

Observations—

1. Why does the hen turn her head first this side and that as she looks at you? Can she see an object with both eyes at once? Can she see well?

2. How many colors are there in a hen's eye? Describe the pupil and the iris.

3. Does the hen wink as we do? Has she any eyelids?

4. Can you see the film lid? Does it come from above or below or the inner or outer corner? When do you see this film lid?

5. Where are the hen's ears? How do they look? How can you tell where the rooster's ears are?

6. Do you think the hen can see and hear well?

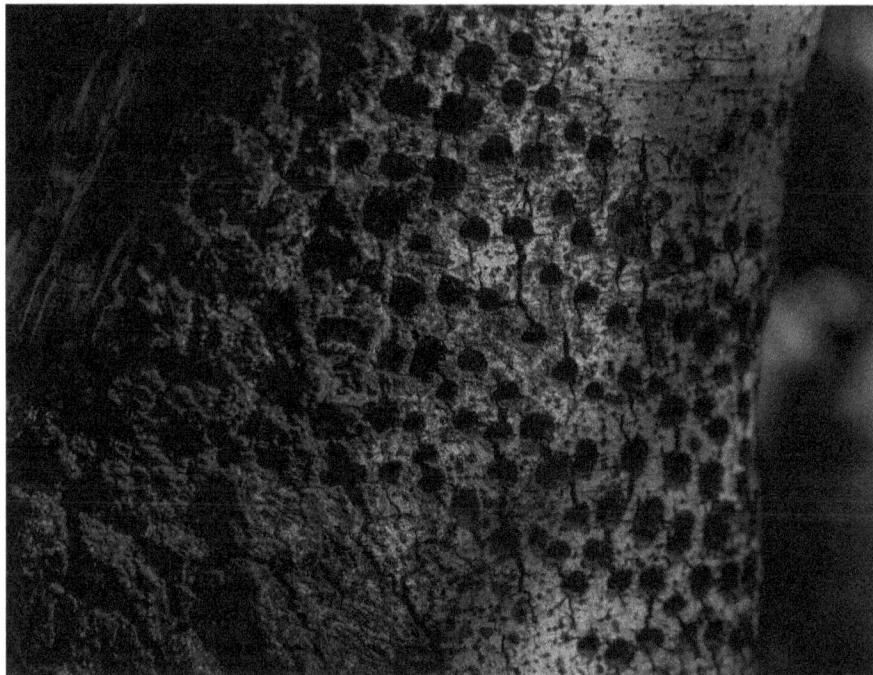

Woodpecker holes in a tree. These were made by a woodpecker in search of insects

The Form and Use of Beaks

SINCE the bird uses its arms and hands for flying, it has been obliged to develop other organs to take their place, and of their work the beak does its full share. It is well to emphasize this point by letting the children at recess play the game of trying to eat an apple or to put up their books and pencils with their arms tied behind them; such an experiment will show how naturally the teeth and feet come to the aid when the hands are useless.

The hen feeds upon seeds and insects which she finds on or in the ground; her beak is horny and sharp and acts not only as a pair of nippers, but also as a pick as she strikes it into the soil to get the seed or insect, having already made bare the place by scratching away the grass or surface of the soil with her strong, stubby toes. The hen does not have any teeth, nor does she need any, for her sharp beak enables her to seize her food; and she does not need to chew it, since her gizzard does this for her after the food is swallowed.

The duck's bill is broad, flat, and much softer than the hen's beak. The duck feeds upon water insects and plants; it attains these by thrusting its head down into the water, seizing the food and holding it fast while the water is strained out through the sieve at the edges of the beak; for this use, a wide, flat beak is necessary. It would be quite as impossible for a duck to pick up hard seeds with its broad, soft bill as it would for the hen to get the duck's food out of the water with her narrow, horny bill.

Both the duck and hen use their bills for cleaning and oiling their feathers and for fighting also; the hen strikes a sharp blow with her beak making a wound like a dagger, while the duck seizes the enemy and simply pinches hard. Both fowls also use their beaks for turning over the eggs when incubating, and also as an aid to the feet when they make nests for themselves.

The nostrils are very noticeable and are situated in the beak near the base. However, we do not believe that birds have a keen sense of smell since their nostrils are not surrounded by a damp, sensitive, soft

SHARP PHOTOGRAPHY (CC BY 4.0)
Black-headed weaver (Ploceus cucullatus bohndorffi) *male building a nest*

surface as are the nostrils of the deer and dog, this arrangement aiding these animals to detect odor in a marvelous manner.

Lesson

Leading thought— Each kind of bird has a beak especially adapted for getting its food. The beak and feet of a bird are its chief weapons and implements.

Methods— Study first the beak of the hen or chick and then that of the duckling or gosling.

Observations—

1. What kind of food does the hen eat and where and how does she find it in the field or garden? How is her beak adapted to get this food? If her beak were soft like that of a duck could she peck so hard for seeds and worms? Has the hen any teeth? Does she need any?

2. Compare the bill of the hen with that of the duck. What are the differences in shape? Which is the harder?

3. Note the saw teeth along the edge of the duck's bill. Are these for chewing? Do they act as a strainer? Why does the duck need to strain its food?

4. Could a duck pick up a hen's food from the earth or the hen strain out a duck's food from the water? For what other things than getting food do these fowls use their bills?

5. Can you see the nostrils in the bill of a hen? Do they show plainer in the duck? Do you think the hen can smell as keenly as the duck?

Supplementary reading— *The Bird Book*, p. 99; *The First Book of Birds*, pp. 95-7; *Mother Nature's Children*, Chapter VIII.

"It is said that nature-study teaching should be accurate, a statement that every good teacher will admit without debate; but accuracy is often interpreted to mean completeness, and then the statement cannot pass unchallenged. To study 'the dandelion,' 'the robin,' with emphasis on the article 'the,' working out the complete structure, may be good laboratory work in botany or zoology for advanced pupils, but it is not an elementary educational process. It contributes nothing more to accuracy than does the natural order of leaving untouched all those phases of the subject that are out of the child's reach; while it may take out the life and spirit of the work, and the spiritual quality may be the very part that is most worth the while. Other work may provide the formal 'drill'; this should supply the quality and vivacity. Teachers often say to me that their children have done excellent work with these complete methods, and they show me the essays and drawings; but this is no proof that the work is commendable. Children can be made to do many things that they ought not to do and that lie beyond them. We all need to go to school to children."

—"THE OUTLOOK TO NATURE," L. H. BAILEY.

"Weather and wind and waning moon,
Plain and hilltop under the sky,
Ev'ning, morning and blazing noon,
Brother of all the world am I.
The pine-tree, linden and the maize,
The insect, squirrel and the kine,
All—natively they live their days—
As they live theirs, so I live mine,
I know not where, I know not what:—
Believing none and doubting none
What'er befalls it counteth not,—
Nature and Time and I are one."

—L. H. BAILEY.

A close-up of a White Cockatoo's feet

The Feet of Birds

OBVIOUSLY, the hen is a digger of the soil; her claws are long, strong and slightly hooked, and her feet and legs are covered with horny scales as a protection from injury when used in scratching the hard earth, in order to lay bare the seeds and insects hiding there. The hen is a very good runner indeed. She lifts her wings a little to help, much as an athletic runner uses his arms, and so can cover ground with amazing rapidity, her strong toes giving her a firm foothold. The track she makes is very characteristic; it consists of three toe-marks projecting forward and one backward. A bird's toes are numbered thus:

A duck has the same number of toes as the hen, but there is a membrane, called the web, which joins the second, third and fourth toes, making a fan-shaped foot; the first or the hind toe has a little web of its own. A webbed foot is first of all a paddle for propelling its owner through the water; it is also a very useful foot on the shores of ponds and streams, since its breadth and flatness prevent it from sinking into the soft mud.

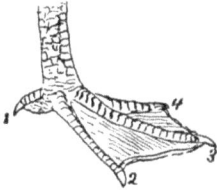

Duck's foot and hen's foot with toes numbered.

The duck's legs are shorter than those of the hen and are placed farther back and wider apart. The reason for this is, they are essentially swimming organs and are not fitted for scratching nor for running. They are placed at the sides of the bird's body so that they may act as paddles, and are farther back so that they may act like the wheel of a propeller in pushing the bird along. We often laugh at a duck on land, since its short legs are so far apart and so far back that its walk is necessarily an awkward waddle; but we must always remember that the duck is naturally a water bird, and on the water its movements are graceful. Think once, how a hen would appear if she attempted to swim! The duck's body is so illy balanced on its short legs that it cannot run rapidly; and if chased even a short distance, will fall dead from the effort, as many a country child has discovered to his sorrow when he tried to drive the ducks home from the creek or pond to coop. The long, hind claw of the hen enables her to clasp a roost firmly during the night; a duck's foot could not do this and the duck sleeps squatting on the ground. However, the Muscovy ducks, which are not good swimmers, have been known to perch.

LESSON

Leading thought— The feet of birds are shaped so as to assist the bird in getting its food as well as for locomotion.

Methods— The pupils should have opportunity to observe the chicken or hen and a duck as they move about; they should also observe the duck swimming.

Observations—

1. Are the toes of the hen long and strong? Have they long, sharp claws at their tips?

2. How are the legs and feet of the hen covered and protected?

3. How are the hen's feet and legs fitted for scratching the earth, and why does she wish to scratch the earth?

4. Can a hen run rapidly? What sort of a track does she make?

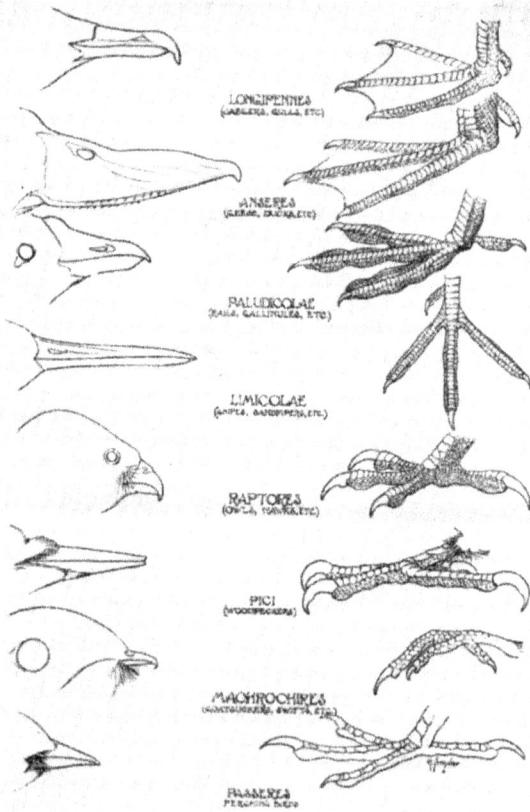

LONGIPENNES
(ALBATROSS, GULLS, ETC.)

ANSERES
(GEESE, DUCKS, ETC.)

PALUDICOLAE
(RAILS, GALLINULES, ETC.)

LIMICOLAE
(SNIPES, SANDPIPERS, ETC.)

RAPTORES
(OWLS, HAWKS, ETC.)

PICI
(WOODPECKERS)

MACROCHIRES
(GOATSUCKERS, SWIFTS, ETC.)

PASSERES
(PERCHING BIRDS)

Types of bills and feet

5. You number your fingers with the thumb as number one and the little finger as five. How do you think the hen's toes are numbered?

6. Has the duck as many toes as the hen? What is the chief difference between the feet of the duck and the hen?

7. Which of the duck's toes are connected by a web? Does the web extend to the tips of the toes? What is the web for and how does it help the duck?

8. Are the duck's legs as long as the hen's? Are they placed farther forward or farther back than those of the hen? Are they farther apart?

9. Can a duck run as well as a hen? Can the hen swim at all?

10. Where does the hen sleep and how does she hold on to her perch? Could the duck hold on to a perch? Does the duck need to perch while sleeping?

Songs of Birds

Anyone who attempts to recognize birds by sight alone misses much of the pleasure that comes to those who have taken the time and pains to learn bird songs and use them as a means of bird recognition. It is true that not all people have a talent for music; but anyone interested in birds can learn to identify the songs and most of the call notes of common birds.

The observer will notice that in most cases only the male bird sings, but a few exceptions are recorded, notably the female rose-breasted grosbeak and cardinal grosbeak, which sing under some conditions. Birds do most of their singing in the early morning and during the spring and early summer months. The male birds have not only a favorite time of day and a particular season of the year during which they do most of their singing, but they even have a certain perch or narrowly defined territory from which they sing.

Each person will need to decide how he can best remember bird songs. Most people will doubtless use such methods as were used by earlier bird students. Long literary descriptions were given for each song. Alexander Wilson, for instance, describes the call of the male blue jay as "repeated creakings of an ungreased wheelbarrow." Often the call of a particular bird is put into words; in many cases these words have come to be accepted as the common name of the bird, such as bobwhite and whip-poor-will. The imagination of students may

Notations.

1. Wood Thrushes.
2. Song Sparrow.
3. Bobolink.
4. Olive-backed Thrush.
5. Meadowlarks.
(Phrase.) (Answer.)

suggest certain words to represent the song or call notes of a bird. These are often more easily remembered than the song itself.

Some ornithologists have developed complicated systems of recording bird songs as musical scores. Wilson Flagg and F. S. Mathews are well-known names in this field. Such a method has its limitations because many variations of bird songs cannot be indicated by the characters used in writing music. The song of a bird written as music is not usually recognizable when played on a musical instrument. Other ornithologists have developed more graphic methods of recording bird songs. One leader in this field, A. A. Saunders, has proposed and used a system employing lines, dots, dashes, and syllables. This system is very interesting and is a useful one to a person who has a good ear for music. One of the latest methods of recording bird songs has been developed by the Department of Ornithology, Cornell University, Ithaca, New York. By this method bird songs are photographed on moving picture film and later may be recorded on phonograph records; these records can be played over and over again to give the student practice in identifying bird songs. Sound pictures have also been produced; the pictures of the various birds are shown on the screen as their songs are being heard by the audience.

SUGGESTED READING - *Bird Friends*, by Gilbert H. Trafton; *Birds and Their Attributes*, by Glover M. Allen; *The Book of Bird Life*, by A. A. Allen;

The Book of Birds, edited by Gilbert Grosvenor and Alexander Wetmore; *Field Book of Wild Birds and Their Music*, by F. Schuyler Mathews; *A Guide to Bird Songs*, by Aretas A. Saunders; *Songs of Wild Birds and More Songs of Wild Birds*, by Albert R. Brand.

A Robin singing

Blue Jays In a Bird Bath

Attracting Birds

If suitable and sufficient food, water, shelter, and nesting sites are provided, and if protection is given from such enemies as cats and thoughtless men, it is possible to attract many kinds of birds to home grounds or gardens. The most logical time to begin to attract birds is during the winter months; but the best time is whenever one is really interested and is willing to provide the things most needed by the birds. Certain types of food, such as suet or sunflower seeds, are sought by birds at any season. During the summer months water for drinking and bathing may be more desired than food, but in the winter almost any seeds, fruits, or fatty foods are welcome.

In the spring nesting boxes properly constructed and placed will do much to attract some kinds of birds, especially those that normally nest in holes in trees. An abundance of choice nesting materials will entice orioles, robins, or chipping sparrows to nest nearby. Straws, sticks, feathers, cotton, strings, or even hairs from old mattresses may be put out as inducements to prospective bird tenants. The spring is also a good time to plant fruit-bearing trees, shrubs, and vines; these natural food counters become more attractive each year as they grow larger and produce more fruit and better nesting places for birds.

Autumn is the ideal time to establish feeding centers to which the birds may be attracted during the winter months. Food, such as suet or seeds, should be put at a great many places throughout the area in which one wishes to attract birds. The birds will gradually work their way from one of these feedings points to another; soon it will be possible to concentrate the feeding at one point, and the birds will continue to come to that point as long as food is provided there.

SUGGESTED READING - *The A B C of Attracting Birds*, by Alvin M. Peterson; *Bird Houses Boys Can Build*, by Albert F. Siepert; *Birds of the Wild - How to Make Your Home Their Home*, by Frank C. Pellett; *Bird Study for Schools Series*, published by the National Association of Audubon Societies (Part III, Winter Feeding, Part IV, Bird Houses); *The Book of Bird Life*, by A. A. Allen; *Boy Bird House Architecture*, by Leon H. Baxter; *The Children's Book of Birds* (First Book of Birds and Second Book of Birds), by Olive Thorne Miller; *Homes for Birds*, by E. R. Kalmbach and W. L. McAtee (U. S. Department of Agriculture, Farmers' Bulletin 1456); *How to Attract Birds in Northeastern United States, How to Attract Birds in Northwestern United States, How to Attract Birds in the Middle Atlantic States, How to Attract Birds in the East Central States*, by W. L. McAtee (U. S. Department of Agriculture, Farmers' Bulletins 621, 760, 844,912); *How to Have Bird Neighbors*, by S. Louise Patteson; *Our Winter Birds*, by Frank M. Chapman; *Permanent Bird Houses*, by Gladstone Califf; *Song-bird Sanctuaries, with Tables of Trees, Shrubs and Vines Attractive to Birds*, by Roger T. Peterson; *Wild Bird Guests*, by Ernest H. Baynes; *Methods of Attracting Birds*, by Gilbert H. Trafton.

Warbling Vireo (Vireo gilvus) *on nest. Vireos live largely on insects gleaned from the under surfaces of leaves and from crevices in bark*

Value of Birds

Did you ever try to calculate in dollars the pleasure that you receive from seeing or hearing the first spring migrants? The robin, bluebird, and meadowlark bring cheer to thousands of people every year. Indeed, it would be difficult to find anyone, except perhaps in large cities, who does not notice the arrival of at least some spring birds—the robins on the lawn, the honk of the wild geese overhead, or the song sparrows as they sing from the top of a shrub. Birds are interesting to most people because of their mere presence, their songs, their colors, or their habits. Persons engaged in nature-study are led outdoors and thus have opened to them many other nature fields.

One needs to observe a bird for only a short time to discover for himself what has been known by scientists for many years, that birds are of great economic importance. Watch a chickadee or nuthatch as it makes its feeding rounds on a winter day. Note how carefully each tiny branch is covered by the chickadee and what a thorough examination of the limbs and trunks is made by the nuthatch. Countless insect eggs as well as insects are consumed. On a sunny day in spring, observe the warblers as they feed about the newly opened leaves and blossoms of the trees. See them as they hunt tirelessly for their quota of the tiny insects so small that they are generally overlooked by larger birds. It must be remembered too that some birds do, at times, take a toll of cultivated crops; this is especially true of the seed-eating and insectivorous birds. But they deserve some pay for the work they do for man, and so in reality he should not begrudge them a little fruit or grain.

Some of the birds of prey are active all the time; the hawks work in the daytime and the owls come on duty for the night shift. Countless destructive small mammals and insects are eaten by them; thus they tend to regulate the numbers of numerous small pests of field and wood, thereby preventing serious outbreaks of such animals. There has been much discussion of the real economic status of hawks and owls; many food studies have been made and the general conclusion is that most species are more useful than harmful. It is true that some species do take a toll of game birds, song birds, and poultry; but they include also in their diet other animal forms, many of which are considered harm-

A winter bird nest with snow

A bluebird outside a birdhouse

ful. One individual bird may be especially destructive and thus give a bad name to an entire species.

There are even garbage gatherers among the birds; vultures, gulls, and crows serve in this capacity. The vultures are commonly found in the warmer parts of the country and serve a most useful purpose by their habit of devouring the unburied bodies of dead animals. The gulls are the scavengers of waterways and shore lines. The crow is omnivorous - that is, it eats both plant and animal food; but it seems to like carrion as well as fresh meat.

The farmer and the gardener owe quite a debt of thanks to the birds that eat weed seeds. Of course there are still bountiful crops of weeds each year; but there would be even more weeds if it were not for the army of such seed-eating birds as sparrows, bobwhites, and doves.

The game birds, such as grouse, pheasant, and bobwhite are important today, chiefly from the standpoint of the recreation they afford sportsmen and other lovers of the outdoors. The food habits of game birds do not present much of an economic problem; the birds are not numerous enough at the present time to be an important source of meat for man as they were in pioneer days.

Thus, a brief consideration of a few types of birds will show even

Hummingbird at feeder

a casual observer that birds have economic importance and that each species seems to have a definite work to perform.

SUGGESTED READING - *Bird Friends*, by Gilbert H. Trafton; *Birds and Their Attributes*, by Glover M. Allen; *Birds in Their Relation to Man*, by Clarence M. Weed and Ned Dearborn; *The Book of Bird Life*, by A. A. Allen; *The Book of Birds*, edited by Gilbert Grosvenor and Alexander Wetmore; *The Children's Book of Birds (First Book of Birds and Second Book of Birds)*, by Olive Thorne Miller; *The Practical Value of Birds*, by Junius Henderson.

LESSON

There are very good reasons for not studying birds' nests in summer, since the birds misinterpret familiarity on the part of eager children and are likely, in consequence, to abandon both nest and locality. But after the birds have gone to sunnier climes and the empty nests are the only mementos we have of them, then we may study these habitations carefully and learn how to appreciate properly the small architects which made them. I think that every one of us who carefully examines the way that a nest is made must have a feeling of respect for its clever little builder.

I know of certain schools where the children make large collections of these winter nests, properly labeling each, and thus gain a new interest in the bird life of their locality. A nest when collected should be labeled in the following manner:

The name of the bird which built the nest.

Where the nest was found. If in a tree, what kind?

How high from the ground?

After a collection of nests has been made, let the pupils study them according to the following outline:

1. Where was the nest found?

    (a) If on the ground, describe the locality.

    (b) If on a plant, tree, or shrub, tell the species, if possible.

    (c) If on a tree, tell where it was on a branch—in a fork, or hanging by the end of the twigs.

    (d) How high from the ground, and what was the locality?

    (e) If on or in a building, how situated?

2. Did the nest have any arrangement to protect it from rain?

3. Give the size of the nest, the diameter of the inside and the outside; also the depth of the inside.

4. What is the form of the nest? Are its sides flaring or straight? Is the nest shaped like a cup, basket, or pocket?

5. What materials compose the outside of the nest and how are they arranged?

6. Of what materials is the lining made, and how are they arranged? If hair or feathers are used, on what creature did they grow?

7. How are the materials of the nest held together, that is, are they woven, plastered, or held in place by environment?

8. Had the nest anything peculiar about it either in situation, construction, or material that would tend to render it invisible to the casual glance?

SUGGESTED READING - *The Book of Bird Life*, by A. A. Allen; *Nature - by Seaside and Wayside*, by Mary G. Phillips and Julia M. Wright, *Book 3, Plants and Animals; Ornithology Laboratory Notebook*, by A. A. Allen; *A Year in the Wonderland of Birds*, by Hallam Hawksworth.

Week old chicks

Chicken Ways

DAME Nature certainly pays close attention to details, and an instance of this is the little tooth on the tip of the upper mandible of the young chick to aid it in breaking out of its egg-shell prison; and since a tooth in this particular place is of no use later, it disappears. The children are delighted with the beauty of a fluffy, little chick with its bright, questioning eyes and its life of activity as soon as it is freed from the shell. What a contrast to the blind, bare, scrawny young robin, which seems to be all mouth! The difference between the two is fundamental since it gives a character for separating ground birds from perching birds. The young partridge, quail, turkey and chick are clothed and active and ready to go with the mother in search of food as soon as they are hatched; while the young of the perching birds are naked and blind, being kept warm by the brooding mother, and fed and nourished by food brought by their parents, until they are large enough to leave the nest. The down which covers the young chick differs from the feathers which come later; the down has no quill but consists of several flossy threads coming from the same root; later on, this down is pushed out and off by the true feathers which grow from the same sockets. The

Chicks and ducklings

pupils should see that the down is so soft that the little, fluffy wings of the chick are useless until the real wing feathers appear.

We chew food until it is soft and fine, then swallow it, but the chick swallows it whole and after being softened by juices from the stomach it passes into a little mill, in which is gravel that the chicken has swallowed, which helps to grind the food. This mill is called the gizzard and the pupils should be taught to look carefully at this organ the next time they have chicken for dinner. A chicken has no muscles in the throat, like ours, to enable it to swallow water as we do. Thus, it has first to fill its beak with water, then hold it up so the water will flow down the throat of itself. As long as the little chick has its mother's wings to sleep under, it does not need to put its head under its own wing; but when it grows up and spends the night upon a roost, it always tucks its head under its wing while sleeping.

The conversation of the barnyard fowl covers many elemental emotions and is easily comprehended. It is well for the children to understand from the first that the notes of birds mean something definite. The hen clucks when she is leading her chicks afield so that they will know where she is in the tall grass; the chicks follow "cheeping" or "peeping," as the children say, so that she will know where they are; but if a chick feels itself lost its "peep" becomes loud and disconsolate; on the other hand, there is no sound in the world so full of cosy contentment as the low notes of the chick as it cuddles under the mother's wing. When a hen finds a bit of food she utters rapid notes which call the chicks in a hurry, and when she sees a hawk she gives a warning "q-r-r" which makes every chick run for cover and keep quiet. When hens are taking their sun and dust baths together, they evidently gossip and we can almost hear them saying, "Did you not think Madam Dorking

A chicken flock with Rhode Island Red, Easter Egger, and Barred Plymouth Rock Hens

made a great fuss over her egg to-day?" Or, "that overgrown young rooster has got a crow to match his legs, has he not?" Contrast these low tones to the song of the hen as she issues forth in the first warm days of spring and gives to the world one of the most joyous songs of all nature. There is quite a different quality in the triumphant cackle of a hen telling to the world that she has laid an egg and the cackle which comes from being startled. When a hen is sitting or is not allowed to sit, she is nervous and irritable and voices her mental state by scolding. When she is really afraid, she squalls and when seized by an enemy, she utters long, horrible squawks. The rooster crows to assure his flock that all is well; he also crows to show other roosters what he thinks of himself and of them. The rooster also has other notes; he will question you as you approach him and his flock, and he will give a warning note when he sees a hawk; when he finds some dainty tidbit he calls his flock of hens to him and they usually arrive just in time to see him swallow the morsel.

When roosters fight, they confront each other with their heads lowered and then try to seize each other by the back of the neck with their beaks, or strike each other with the wing spurs, or tear with the leg spurs. Weasels, skunks, rats, hawks and crows are the most common enemies of the fowls, and often a rooster will attack one of these invaders and fight valiantly; the hen will also fight if her brood is disturbed.

LESSON

Leading thought— Chickens have interesting habits of life and extensive conversational powers.

Method— For this lesson it is necessary that the pupils observe the inhabitants of the poultry yard and answer these questions a few at a time.

Observations—

1. Did the chick get out of the egg by its own efforts? For what use is the little tooth which is on the tip of the upper part of a young chicken's beak? Does this remain?

2. What is the difference between the down of the chick and the feathers of the hen? The little chick has wings; why can it not fly?

3. Why is the chick just hatched so pretty and downy, while the young robin is so bare and ugly? Why is the young chick able to see while the young robin is blind?

4. How does the young chick get its food?

5. Does the chick chew its food before swallowing? If not, why?

6. How does the chick drink? Why does it drink this way?

7. Where does the chick sleep at night? Where will it sleep when it is grown up?

8. Where does the hen put her head when she is sleeping?

9. How does the hen call her chicks when she is with them in the field?

10. How does she call them to food?

11. How does she tell them that there is a hawk in sight?

12. What notes does the chick make when it is following its mother? When it gets lost? When it cuddles under her wing?

13. What does the hen say when she has laid an egg? When she is frightened? When she is disturbed while sitting on eggs? When she is grasped by an enemy? How do hens talk together? Describe a hen's song.

14. When does the rooster crow? What other sounds does he make?

15. With what weapons does the rooster fight his rivals and his enemies?

16. What are the natural enemies of the barnyard fowls and how do they escape them?

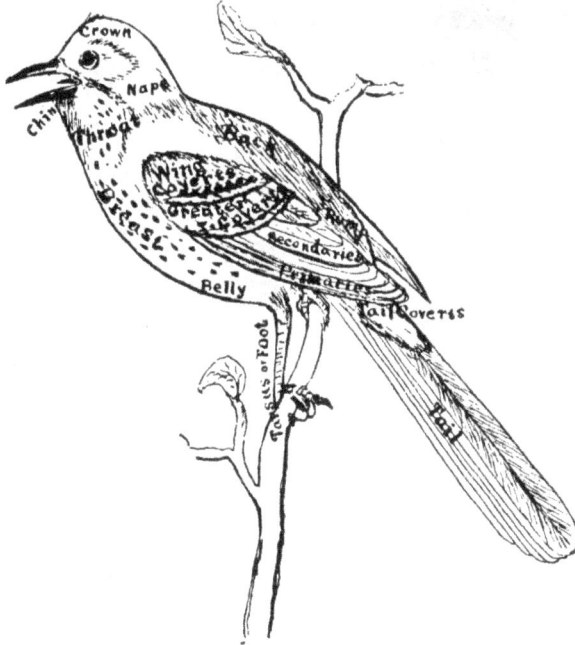

Parts of the bird labeled.

This figure should be placed on the blackboard where pupils may consult it when studying colors and markings of birds.

Supplementary reading— *True Bird Stories*, Miller p. 102.

Pigeon House

Pigeons

THERE is a mention of domesticated pigeons by writers three thousand years ago; and Pliny relates that the Romans were fervent pigeon fanciers at the beginning of the Christian era. All of our domestic varieties of pigeons have been developed from the Rock pigeon, a wild species common in Europe and Asia. The carrier pigeon was probably the first to be specially developed because of its usefulness; its love and devotion to mate and young and its homesickness when separated from them were used by man for his own interests. When a knight of old started off on a Crusade or to other wars, he took with him several pigeons from the home cote; and after riding many days he wrote a letter and tied it to the neck or under the wing of one of his birds, which he then set free, and it flew home with its message; later he would set free another in like manner. The drawback to this correspondence was that it went only in one direction; no bird from home brought message of cheer to the wandering knight. Now-a-days mail routes, telegraph wires and wireless currents enmesh our globe

48

and the pigeon as a carrier is out-of-date; but fanciers still perfect the homer breed and train pigeons for very difficult flight competitions, some of them a distance of hundreds of miles. Recently a homer made one thousand miles in two days, five hours and fifty minutes. Read to the pupils "Arnaux" in Animal Heroes by Thompson Seton to give them an idea of the life of a homing pigeon.

The natural food of pigeons is grain; we feed them cracked corn, wheat, peas, Kafir corn, millet and occasionally hemp seed; it is best to feed mixed rations as the birds tire of the monotonous diet. Pigeons should be fed twice a day; the pigeon is the only bird which can drink like a horse, that is, with the head lowered. The walk of a pigeon is accompanied by a peculiar nodding as if the head were in some way attached to the feet, and this movement sends waves of iridescent colors over the bird's plumage. The flight of the pigeon is direct without soaring, the wings move rapidly and steadily, the birds circling and sailing as they start or alight. The crow flaps hard and then sails for a distance when it is inspecting the ground, while the hawk soars on motionless wings. It requires closer attention to understand the language of the pigeon than that of the hen, nor has it so wide a range of expression as the latter; however, some emotions are voiced in the cooing, which the children will understand.

The nest is built of grass and twigs; the mother pigeon lays two eggs for a sitting; but in some breeds a pair will raise from seven to

Pigmy Pouter Pigeon

twelve broods per year. The eggs hatch in from sixteen to eighteen days, and both parents share the labors of incubating. In the case of the homer the father bird sits from 10 A. M. to 4 P. M. and the mother the remainder of the day and night. The devotion of pigeons to their mates and to their young is great, and has been sung by the poets and praised by the philosophers during many ages; some breeds mate for life. The young pigeons or squabs are fed in a peculiar manner; in the crops of both parents is secreted a cheesy substance, known as pigeon milk. The parent seizes the beak of the squab in its own and pumps the food from its own crop into the stomach of the young. This nutritious food is given to the squab for about five days and then replaced by grain which is softened in the parents' stomachs, until the squabs are old enough to feed themselves. Rats, mice, weasels, and hawks are the chief enemies of the pigeons; since pigeons cannot fight, their only safety lies in flight.

As the original Rock pigeon built in caves, our domesticated varieties naturally build in the houses we provide for them. A pigeon house should not be built for more than fifty pairs; it should be well ventilated and kept clean; it should face the south or east and be near a shallow, running stream if possible. The nest boxes should be twelve inches square and nine inches in height with a door at one side, so that the nest may remain hidden. In front of each door there should be a little shelf to act as a balcony on which the resting parent bird may sit and coo to relieve the monotony of the sitter. Some breeders make a double compartment instead of providing a balcony, while in Egypt branches are inserted in the wall just below the doors of the very ornamental pigeon houses. The houses should be kept clean and whitewashed with lime to which carbolic acid is added in the proportion of one tea-spoonful of acid to two gallons of the wash; the leaf stems of tobacco should be given to the pigeons as material for building their nests, so as to help keep in check the bird lice. There should be near the pigeon house plenty of fresh water for drinking and bathing; also a box of table salt, and another of cracked oyster shell and another of charcoal as fine as ground coffee. Salt is very essential to the health of pigeons. The house should be high enough from the ground to keep the inmates safe from rats and weasels.

LESSON

Leading thought— The pigeons differ in appearance from other birds and also in their actions. Their nesting habits are very interesting and there are many things that may be done to make the pigeons comfortable. They were, in ancient days, used as letter carriers.

Methods— If there are pigeons kept in the neighborhood, it is best to encourage the pupils to observe these birds out-of-doors. Begin the work with an interesting story and with a few questions which will arouse the pupils' interest in the birds. A pigeon in a cage in the schoolroom for a special lesson on the bird's appearance, is desirable but not necessary.

Observations—

1. For an out-of-door exercise during recess let the pupils observe the pigeon and tell the colors of the beak, eyes, top of the head, back, breast, wings, tail, feet and claws. This exercise is excellent training to fit the pupils to note quickly the colors of the wild birds.

2. On what do pigeons feed? Are they fond of salt?

3. Describe how a pigeon drinks. How does it differ in this respect from other birds?

4. Describe the peculiar movement of the pigeon when walking.

5. Describe the pigeon's flight. Is it rapid, high in the air, do the wings flap constantly, etc? What is the chief difference between the flight of pigeons, crows or hawks?

6. Listen to the cooing of a pigeon and see if you can understand

A domestic pigeon

the different notes.

7. Describe the pigeon's nest. How many eggs are laid at a time?

8. Describe how the parents share the labors in hatching the eggs, and how long after the eggs are laid before the young hatch?

9. How do the parents feed their young and on what material?

10. What are the enemies of pigeons and how do they escape from them? How can we protect them?

11. Describe how a pigeon house should be built.

12. What must you do for pigeons to keep them healthy and comfortable?

13. How many breeds of pigeons do you know? Describe them.

Supplementary reading— "Arnaux" in *Animal Heroes*, Thompson Seton; Audubon Leaflet, Nos. 2 and 6; *Neighbors with Wings and Fins* Ch. XV; *Noah and the Dove*, The Bible; *Daddy Darwin's Dove Cote*, Mrs. Ewing; *Squab Raising*, Bul. of U. S. Dept. Agr.

For my own part I readily concur with you in supposing that housedoves are derived from the small blue rock-pigeon, Columba livia, for many reasons…

But what is worth a hundred arguments is, the instance you give in Sir Roger Mostyn's housedoves in Caernarvonshire; which, though tempted by plenty of food and gentle treatment, can never be prevailed on to inhabit their cote for any time; but as soon as they begin to breed, betake themselves to the fastnesses of Ormshead, and deposit their young in safety amidst the inaccessible caverns and precipices of that stupendous promontory. "You may drive nature out with a pitchfork, but she will always return:" "Naturam expellas furca... tamen usque recurret."

Virgil, as a familiar occurrence, by way of simile, describes a dove haunting the cavern of a rock in such engaging numbers, that I cannot refrain from quoting the passage.

> "Qualis spelunca subito commota Columba,
> Cui domus, et dulces latebroso in pumice nidi,
> Fertul in arva volans, plausumque exterrita pennis
> Dat tecto ingentem, mox aere lapsa quieto,
> Radit iter liquidum, celeres neque commovet alas."
>
> (VIRG. AEN. V. 213-217).

> "As when a dove her rocky hold forsakes,
> Roused, in a fright her sounding wings she shakes;
> The cavern rings with clattering:—out she flies,
> And leaves her callow care, and cleaves the skies;
> At first she flutters:—but at length she springs
> To smoother flight, and shoots upon her wings."
>
> (DRYDEN'S TRANSLATION).
>
> WHITE OF SELBOURNE.

A goldfinch pair

The Canary and the Goldfinch

TEACHER'S STORY

IN childhood the language of birds and animals is learned unconsciously. What child, who cares for a canary, does not understand its notes which mean loneliness, hunger, eagerness, joy, scolding, fright, love and song!

The pair of canaries found in most cages are not natural mates. The union is one *de convenance,* forced upon them by people who know little of bird affinities. We could hardly expect that such a mating would be always happy. The singer, as the male is called, is usually arbitrary and tyrannical and does not hesitate to lay chastising beak upon his spouse. The expression of affection of the two is usually very practical, consisting of feeding each other with many beguiling notes and much fluttering of wings. The singer may have several songs; whether he has many or few depends upon his education; he usually shows exultation when singing by throwing the head back like a prima-donna, to let the music well forth. He is usually brighter yellow in color with more brilliantly black markings than his mate; she usually has much gray in her plumage. But there are about fifty varieties of canaries and each has distinct color and markings.

Canaries should be given a more varied diet than most people think. The seeds we buy or that we gather from the plantain or wild grasses, they eat eagerly. They like fresh, green leaves of lettuce and chickweed and other tender herbage; they enjoy bread and milk occasionally. There should always be a piece of cuttle-fish bone or sand and gravel where they can get it, as they need grit for digestion. Above all, they should have fresh water. Hard-boiled egg is given them while nesting. The canary seed which we buy for them is the product of a grass in the Canary Islands. Hemp and rape seed are also sold for canary food.

The canary's beak is wide and sharp and fitted for shelling seeds; it is not a beak fitted for capturing insects. The canary, when drinking, does not have to lift the beak so high in the air in order to swallow the water as do some birds. The nostrils are in the beak and are easily seen; the ear is hidden by the feathers. The canary is a fascinating little creature when it shows interest in an object; it has such a knowing look, and its perfectly round, black eyes are so intelligent and cunning. If the canary winks, the act is so rapid as to be seen with difficulty, but when drowsy, the little inner lid appears at the inner corner of its eye and the outer lids close so that we may be sure that they are there; the lower lid covers more of the eye than the upper.

The legs and toes are covered with scale armor; the toes have long, curved claws that are neither strong nor sharp but are especially fitted for holding to the perch; the long hind toe with its stronger claw makes complete the grasp on the twig. When the canary is hopping about on the bottom of the cage we can see that its toes are more fitted for holding to the perch than for walking.

When the canary bathes, it ducks its head and makes a great splashing with its wings and likes to get thoroughly wet. Afterward, it sits all bedraggled and "humped up" for a time and then usually preens its feathers as they dry. When going to sleep, it at first fluffs out its feathers and squats on the perch, draws back its head and looks very drowsy. Later it tucks its head under its wing for the night and then looks like a little ball of feathers on the perch.

Canaries make a great fuss when building their nest. A pasteboard box is usually given them with cotton and string for lining; usually one pulls out what the other puts in; and they both industriously tear the paper from the bottom of the cage to add to their building material. Finally, a make-shift of a nest is completed and the eggs are laid. If the singer is a good husband, he helps incubate the eggs and feeds his mate and sings to her frequently; but often he is quite the reverse and abuses her abominably. The nest of the caged bird is very different in appearance from the neat nests of grass, plant down, and moss which the wild ancestors of these birds made in some safe retreat in the shrubs or evergreens of the Canary Islands. The canary eggs are pale blue, marked with reddish-brown. The incubation period is 13 to 14 days. The young are as scrawny and ugly as most little birds and are fed upon food partially digested in the parents' stomachs. Their first plumage resembles that of the mother usually.

In their wild state in the Canary and Azore Islands, the canaries are olive green above with golden yellow breasts. When the heat of spring begins, they move up the mountains to cooler levels and come down again in the winter. They may rear three or four broods on their way up the mountains, stopping at successive heights as the season advances, until finally they reach the high peaks.

THE GOLDFINCH OR THISTLE BIRD

The goldfinches are bird midgets but their songs are so sweet and reedy that they seem to fill the world with music more effectually than many larger birds. They are fond of the seeds of wild grass, and especially so of thistle seed; and they throng the pastures and fence corners where the thistles hold sway. In summer, the male has bright yellow plumage with a little black cap "pulled down over his nose" like that of a grenadier. He has also a black tail and wings with white-tipped coverts and primaries. The tail feathers have white on their inner webs also, which does not show when the tail is closed. The female has the head and back brown and the under parts yellowish white, with wings and tail resembling those of the male except that they are not so vividly black. In winter the male dons a dress more like that of his mate; he loses his black cap but keeps his black wings and tail.

A female goldfinch

The song of the goldfinch is exquisite and he sings during the entire period of his golden dress; he sings while flying as well as when at rest. The flight is in itself beautiful, being wave-like up and down, in graceful curves. Mr. Chapman says when on the down half of the curve the male sings "Per-chick or-ree." The goldfinch's call notes and alarm notes are very much like those of the canary.

Since the goldfinches live so largely upon seeds of grasses, they stay with us in small numbers during the winter. During this period both parents and young are dressed in olive green, and their sweet call notes are a surprise to us of a cold, snowy morning, for they are associated in our memory with summer. The male dons his winter suit in October.

The goldfinch nest is a mass of fluffiness. These are the only birds that make feather beds for their young. But, perhaps, we should say beds of down, since it is the thistle down which is used for this mattress. The outside of the nest consists of fine shreds of bark or fine grass closely woven; but the inner portion is a mat of thistle down—an inch and a half thick of cushion for a nest which has an opening of scarcely three inches; sometimes the outside is ornamented with lichens. The nest is usually placed in some bush or tree, often in an evergreen, and not more than 5 or 6 feet from the ground; but sometimes it is placed 30 feet high. The eggs are from four to six in number and bluish white in color. The female builds the nest, her mate cheering her with song meanwhile; he feeds her while she is incubating and helps feed

Goldfinch eggs

the young. A strange thing about the nesting habits of the goldfinches is that the nest is not built until August. It has been surmised that this nesting season is delayed until there is an abundance of thistle down for building material. Audubon Leaflet No. 17 gives special information about these birds and also furnishes an outline of the birds for the pupils to color.

LESSON

Leading thought— The canary is a very close relative of the common wild goldfinch. If we compare the habits of the two we can understand how a canary might live if it were free.

Method— Bring a canary to the schoolroom and ask for observations. Request the pupils to compare the canary with the goldfinches which are common in the summer. The canary offers opportunity for very close observation which will prove excellent training for the pupils for beginning bird study.

Observations—

1. If there are two canaries in the cage are they always pleasant to each other? Which one is the "boss?" How do they show displeasure or bad temper? How do they show affection for each other?

2. Which one is the singer? Does the other one ever attempt to sing? What other notes do the canaries make besides singing? How do they greet you when you bring their food? What do they say when they are lonesome and hungry?

3. Does the singer have more than one song? How does he act while singing? Why does he throw back his head like an opera singer when singing?

4. Are the canaries all the same color? What is the difference in color between the singer and the mother bird? Describe the colors of each in your note book as follows: Top and sides of head, back, tail, wings, throat, breast and under parts?

5. What does the canary eat? What sort of seeds do we buy for it? What seeds do we gather for it in our garden? Do the goldfinches live on the same seeds? What does the canary do to the seeds before eating them? What tools does he use to take off the shells?

6. Notice the shape of the canary's beak. Is it long and strong like a robin's? Is it wide and sharp so that it can shell seeds? If you should put an insect in the cage would the canary eat it?

7. Why do we give the canary cuttlebone? Note how it takes off pieces of the bone. Could it do this if its beak were not sharp?

8. Note the actions of the birds when they drink. Why do they do this?

9. Can you see the nostrils? Where are they situated? Why can you not see the ear?

10. When the canary is interested in looking at a thing how does it act? Look closely at its eyes. Does it wink? How does it close its eyes? When it is drowsy can you see the little inner lid come from the corner of the eye nearest the beak? Is this the only lid?

11. How are the legs and feet covered? Describe the toes. Compare the length of the claw with the length of the toe. What is the shape of the claw? Do you think that such shaped claws and feet are better fitted for holding to a branch than for walking? Note the arrangement of the toes when the bird is on its perch. Is the hind toe longer and stronger? If so, why? Do the canaries hop or walk about the bottom of the cage?

12. What is the attitude of the canary when it goes to sleep at night? How does it act when it takes a bath? How does it get the water over its head? Over its back? What does it do after the bath? If we forget to put in the bath dish how does the bird get its bath?

NESTING HABITS TO BE OBSERVED IN THE SPRING

13. When the canaries are ready to build a nest what material do we furnish them for it? Does the father bird help the mother to build

the nest? Do they strip off the paper on the bottom of the cage for nest material? Describe the nest when it is finished.

14. Describe the eggs carefully. Does the father bird assist in sitting on the eggs? Does he feed the mother bird when she is sitting?

15. How long after the eggs are laid before the young ones hatch? Do both parents feed the young? Do they swallow the food first and partially digest it before giving it to the young?

16. How do the very young birds look? What is their appearance when they leave the nest? Does the color of their plumage resemble that of the father or the mother?

17. Where did the canaries originally come from? Find the place on the map.

Supplementary reading— "A Caged Bird," Sarah Orne Jewett in *Songs of Nature*, p. 75; *True Bird Stories*, Miller.

THE GOLDFINCH

Leading thought— Goldfinches are seen at their best in late summer or September when they appear in flocks wherever the thistle seeds are found in abundance. Goldfinches so resemble the canaries in form, color, song and habits that they are called wild canaries.

Method— The questions for this lesson should be given to the pupils before the end of school in June. The answers to the questions should be put in their field note-books and the results be reported to the teacher in class when the school begins in the autumn.

Observations—

1. Where do you find the goldfinches feeding? How can you distinguish the father from the mother birds and from the young ones in color?

2. Describe the colors of the male goldfinch and also of the female as follows: Crown, back of head, back, tail, wings, throat, breast and lower parts. Describe in particular the black cap of the male.

3. Do you know the song of the goldfinch? Is it like the song of the canary? What other notes has the goldfinch?

4. Describe the peculiar flight of the goldfinches. Do they fly high

in the air? Do you see them singly or in flocks usually?

5. Where do the goldfinches stay during the winter? What change takes place in the coat of the male during the winter? Why? What do they live upon during the winter?

6. At what time of year do the goldfinches build their nests? Why do they build these so much later than other birds? Describe the nest. Where is it placed? How far above the ground? How far from a stream or other water? Of what is the outside made? The lining? What is the general appearance of the nest? Do you think the goldfinches wait until the thistles are ripe in order to gather plenty of food for their young, or to get the thistle down for their nests? What is the color of the eggs?

Supplementary reading— *True Bird Stories*, Miller, pp. 6, 9, 26, 45. *The Second Book of Birds*, Miller, p. 82; *Our Birds and Their Nestlings*, Walker, pp. 180, 200.

Sometimes goldfinches one by one will drop
From low-hung branches; little space they stop,
But sip, and twitter, and their feathers sleek,
Then off at once, as in a wanton freak;
Or perhaps, to show their black and golden wings;
Pausing upon their yellow flutterings.

—JOHN KEATS.

An American Robin

The Robin

MOST of us think we know the robin well, but very few of us know definitely the habits of this, our commonest bird. The object of this lesson is to form in the pupils a habit of careful observation, and enable them to read for themselves the interesting story of this little life which is lived every year before their eyes. Moreover, a robin notebook, if well kept, is a treasure for any child; and the close observation necessary for this lesson trains the pupils to note in a comprehending way the habits of other birds. It is the very best preparation for bird study of the right sort.

A few robins occasionally find a swamp where they can obtain food to nourish them during the northern winter, but for the most part, they go in flocks to our Southern States where they settle in swamps and cedar forests and live upon berries. They are killed in great numbers by the native hunters who eat them or sell them for table use, a performance not understandable to the northerner. The robins do not nest nor sing while in Southland, and no wonder! When the robins first come to us in the spring they feed on wild berries, being especially fond of those of the Virginia creeper. As soon as the frost is out of the ground they begin feeding on earthworms, cutworms, white grubs, and other insects. The male robins come first, but do not sing until their mates arrive.

The robin is ten inches long and the English sparrow is only six and one-third inches long; the pupils should get the sizes of these two birds fixed in their minds for comparison in measuring other birds. The father robin is much more decided in color than his mate; his beak is yellow, there is a yellow ring about the eye and a white spot above it. The head is black and the back slaty-brown; the breast is brilliant reddish brown or bay and the throat is white, streaked with black. The mother bird has paler back and breast and has no black upon the head. The wings of both are a little darker than the back, the tail is black with the two outer feathers tipped with white. These white spots do not show except when the bird is flying and are "call colors," that is, they enable the birds to see each other and thus keep together when flying in flocks during the night. The white patch made by the under tail-coverts serves a similar purpose. The feet and legs are strong and dark in color.

The robin has many sweet songs and he may be heard in the earliest dawn and also in the evenings; if he wishes to cheer his mate he may burst into song at any time. He feels especially songful before the summer showers when he seems to sing, "I have a theory, a theory, it's going to rain." And he might well say that he also has a theory, based on experience, that a soaking shower will drive many of the worms and larvae in the soil up to the surface where he can get them. Besides these songs the robins have a great variety of notes which the female shares, although she is not a singer. The agonizing, angry cries they utter when they see a cat or squirrel must express their feelings fully; while they give a very different warning note when they see crow or hawk, a note hard to describe, but which is a long, not very loud squeak.

A robin can run or hop as pleases him best, and it is interesting to

A newly hatched American robin among unhatched eggs in a nest in Charlotte, North Carolina.

see one, while hunting earthworms, run a little distance, then stop to bend the head and listen for his prey, and when he finally seizes the earthworm he braces himself on his strong legs and tugs manfully until he sometimes almost falls over backward as the worm lets go its hold. The robins, especially at nesting time, eat many insects as well as earthworms.

The beginning of a robin's nest is very interesting; much strong grass, fine straw, leaves and rootlets are brought and placed on a secure support. When enough of this material is collected and arranged, the bird goes to the nearest mud puddle or stream margin and fills its beak with soft mud and going back "peppers" it into the nest material, and after the latter is soaked the bird gets into it and molds it to the body by nestling and turning around and around. In one case which the author watched the mother bird did this part of the building, although the father worked industriously in bringing the other materials. After the nest is molded but not yet hardened, it is lined with fine grass or rootlets. If the season is very dry and there is no soft mud at hand, the robins can build without the aid of this plaster. There are usually four eggs laid which are exquisite greenish blue in color.

Both parents share the monotonous business of incubating, and in the instance under the eyes of the author the mother bird was on the nest at night; the period of incubating is from eleven to fourteen days. The most noticeable thing about a very young robin is its wide, yellow-margined mouth, which it opens like a satchel every time the nest is jarred. This wide mouth cannot but suggest to anyone that it is meant to be stuffed, and the two parents work very hard to fill it. Both parents feed the young and often the father feeds the mother bird while she is brooding. Professor Treadwell experimented

A robin feeding its hungry young

with young robins and found that each would take 68 earthworms daily; these worms if laid end to end would measure about 14 feet. Think of 14 feet of earthworm being wound into the little being in the nest, no wonder that it grows so fast! I am convinced that each pair of robins about our house has its own special territory for hunting worms, and that any trespasser is quickly driven off. The young bird's eyes are unsealed when they are from six to eight days old, and by that time the feather tracts, that is, the place where the feathers are to grow, are covered by the spine-like pin-feathers; these feathers push the down out and it often clings to their tips. In eleven days the birds are pretty well feathered; their wing feathers are fairly developed but alas, they have no tail feathers! When a young robin flies from the nest he is a very uncertain and tippy youngster, not having any tail to steer him while flying, nor to balance him when alighting.

It is an anxious time for the old robins when the young ones leave the nest, and they flutter about and scold at any one who comes in

Young robins. Their spotted breasts show their relationship to the thrushes

sight, so afraid are they that injury will come to their inexperienced young ones; for some time the parents care for the fledglings, solicitously feeding them and giving them warnings of danger. The young robin shows in its plumage its relation to the thrush family, for it is yellowish and very spotted and speckled, especially the breast. The parents may raise several broods, but they never use the same nest for two consecutive broods, both because it may be infested with parasites and because it is more or less soiled; although the mother robin works hard to keep it clean, carrying away all waste matter in her beak and dropping it. Robins do not sing much after the breeding season is over until after they have molted. They are fond of cherries and other pulp fruits and often do much damage to such crops. The wise orchardist will plant a few Russian mulberry trees at a reasonable distance from his cherry trees, and thus, by giving the robins a fruit which they like better, and which ripens a little earlier, he may save his cherries. It has been proven conclusively that the robins are far more beneficial than damaging to the farmer; they destroy many noxious insects, two-thirds of their food the entire year consisting of insects; during April and May they do a great work in destroying cutworms.

The robins stay with us later than most migrating birds, not leaving us entirely before November. Their chief enemies in northern climates are cats, crows and squirrels. Cats should be taught to let birds alone (see lesson on cat) or should be killed. The crows have driven the robins into villages where they can build their nests under the protection of man. If crows venture near a house to attack the robins, firing a gun at them once or twice will give them a hint which they are not slow to take. The robins of an entire neighborhood will attack a nest-robbing crow, but usually too late to save the nestlings. The robins can defend themselves fairly well against the red squirrel unless he steals the contents of the nest while the owners are away. There can be no doubt that the same pair of robins return to the same nesting place year after year. On the Cornell Campus a robin lacking the white tip on one side of his tail was noted to have returned to the same particular feeding ground for several years; and we are very certain that the same female bird built in the vines of our piazza for seven consecutive years; it took two years to win her confidence; but after that, she seemed to feel as if she were a part of the family and regarded us all as friends. We were sure that during her fifth year she brought a new young husband to the old nesting site; probably her faithful old husband had been served for a dinner in some Tennessee hotel during the previous winter.

LESSON

Leading thought— To understand all we can about the life and ways of the robin.

Methods— For first and second grades this work may be done by means of an extra blackboard, or what is far better, sheets of ordinary, buff, manilla wrapping paper fastened together at the upper end, so that they may be hung and turned over like a calendar. On the outside page make a picture of a robin in colored chalk or crayons, coloring according to the children's answers to questions of series "*b*". Devote each page to one series of questions, as given below. Do not show these questions to the pupils until the time is ripe for the observations. Those pupils giving accurate answers to these questions should have their names on a roll of honor on the last page of the chart.

For third or higher grades the pupils should have individual note-books in which each one may write his own answers to the questions of the successive series, which should be written on the blackboard at proper time for the observations. This note-book should have a page about 6x8 inches and may be made of any blank paper. The cover or first page should show the picture of the robin colored by the pupil, and may contain other illustrative drawings, and any poems or other literature pertinent to the subject. If prizes are awarded in the school, a bird book should be given as award for the best note-book in the class.

Observations by pupils—

Series A (To be given in March).

1. At what date did you see the first robin this year?
2. Where did the robin spend the winter; did it build a nest or sing when in its winter quarters?
3. What does it find to eat when it first comes in the spring? How does this differ from its ordinary food?
4. Does the robin begin to sing as soon as it comes North?

Series B (To be given the first week of April).

1. How large is the robin compared with the English sparrow?
2. What is the color of the beak? The eye? Around and above the eye?
3. The color of the top of the head? The back? The throat? The breast?
4. Do all the robins have equally bright colors on head, back and breast?
5. What is the color of the wing feathers?
6. What is the color of the tail feathers? Where is the white on them? Can the white spots be seen except during flight of the bird? Of what use to the robin are these spots?
7. Is there white on the underside of the robin as it flies over you? Where?
8. What is the color of the feet and legs?

SERIES C (TO BE GIVEN THE SECOND WEEK OF APRIL).

1. At what time of day does the robin sing? Is it likely to sing before a rain? How many different songs does a robin sing?

2. What note does a robin give when it sees a cat?

3. What sounds do the robins make when they see a crow or a hawk?

4. Does a robin run or walk or hop?

5. Do you think it finds the hidden earthworm by listening? If so describe the act.

6. Describe how a robin acts as it pulls a big earthworm out of the ground.

7. Do robins eat other food than earthworms?

SERIES D (TO BE GIVEN BY THE MIDDLE OF APRIL).

1. At what date did your pair of robins begin to build their nest?

2. Where was the nest placed and with what material was it begun?

3. Can you tell the difference in colors between the father and mother birds? Do both parents help in making the nest?

4. How and with what material is the plastering done? How is the nest molded into shape? Do both birds do this part of the work?

5. Where is the mud obtained and how carried to the nest?

6. How is the nest lined?

SERIES E (TO BE GIVEN A WEEK AFTER SERIES D).

1. What is the number and color of the eggs in the nest?

2. Do both parents do the sitting? Which sits on the nest during the night?

3. Give the date when the first nestling hatches.

4. How does the young robin look? The color and size of its beak? Why is its beak so large? Can it see? Is it covered with down? Compare it to a young chick and describe the difference between the two.

5. What does the young robin do if it feels any jar against the nest? Why does it do this?

6. Do the young robins make any noise?

7. What do the parents feed their young? Do both parents feed them? Are the young fed in turns?

8. Does each pair of robins have a certain territory for hunting worms which is not trespassed upon by other robins?

SERIES F (TO BE GIVEN THREE DAYS AFTER SERIES E).

1. How long after hatching before the young robin's eyes are open? Can you see where the feathers are going to grow? How do the young feathers look?

2. How long after hatching before the young birds are covered with feathers?

3. Do their wing or tail feathers come first?

4. How is the nest kept clean?

5. Give the date when the young robins leave the nest. How do the old robins act at this important crisis?

6. Describe the young robin's flight. Why is it so unsteady?

7. How do the young robins differ in colors of breast from the parents?

8. Do the parents stay with the young for a time? What care do they give them?

9. If the parents raise a second brood do they use the same nest?

SERIES G (TO BE GIVEN FOR SUMMER READING AND OBSERVATIONS).

1. Do the robins sing all summer? Why?

2. Do the robins take your berries and cherries? How can you prevent them from doing this?

3. How does the robin help us?

4. How long does it stay with us in the fall?

5. What are the chief enemies of the robin and how does it fight or escape them? How can we help protect it?

6. Do you think the same robins come back to us each year?

Supplementary reading— *Nestlings of Forest and Marsh*, Wheelock, p. 62; *Our Birds and their Nestlings*, Walker, pp. 26, 37, 41, 42; *True Bird Stories*, Miller, pp. 37, 138; *The Bird Book*, Eckstrom, p. 248; *Familiar Wild Animals*, Lottridge; *The History of the Robins*, Trimmer; *Field Book of Wild Birds and their Music*, Mathews, p. 246; *Birds in Their Relation to Man*, Weed and Dearborn, p. 90; *Songs of Nature*, Burroughs, p. 94; *Wake Robin*, Burroughs; Audubon Leaflet No. 4.

A pair of Eastern Bluebirds in Michigan, USA.

The Bluebird

TEACHER'S STORY

STERN as were our Pilgrim Fathers, they could not fail to welcome certain birds with plumage the color of June skies, whose sweet voices brought hope and cheer to their homesick hearts at the close of that first, long, hard winter of 1621. The red breasts of these birds brought to memory the robins of old England and so they were called "Blue robins"; and this name expresses well the relationship implied, because the bluebirds and robins of America are both members of the thrush family, a family noted for exquisite song.

The bluebirds are usually ahead of the robins in the northward journey and arrive in New York often amid the blizzards of early March, their soft, rich "curly" notes bringing, even to the doubting mind, glad convictions of coming spring. There is a family resemblance between voices of bluebird and robin, a certain rich quality of tone, but the robin's song is far more assertive and complex than is the soft, "purling" song of the bluebird, which has been vocalized as "tru-al-ly, tru-al-ly." These love songs cease with the hard work of feeding the nestlings in April, but may be heard again as a prelude to the second brood in June. The red breast of the bluebird is its only color resemblance to the robin, although the young bluebirds and robins are both spotted, showing the thrush colors. The robin is so much larger than the bluebird that commonly the relationship is not noticed. This is easily explained because there is

A hollow fence post is a common home of the bluebird. The young are fed chiefly on insects

nothing to suggest a robin in the exquisite cerulean blue of the bluebird's head, back, tail and wings. This color is most brilliant when the bird is on the wing, in the sunshine. However, there is a certain mirror-like quality in these blue feathers; and among leaf shadows or even among bare branches they in a measure, reflect the surroundings and render the bird less noticeable. The female is paler, being grayish blue above and with only a tinge of red-brown on the breast; both birds are white beneath.

The bluebirds haunt open woods, fields of second growth and especially old orchards. They flit about in companies of three or four until they mate for nesting. While feeding, the bluebird usually sits on a low branch keeping a keen eye on the ground below, now and then dropping suddenly on an unsuspecting insect and then returning to its perch; it does not remain on the ground hunting food as does the robin. The nest is usually built in a hole in a tree or post and is made of soft grass. A hollow apple tree is a favorite nesting site.

In building birdhouses we should bear in mind that a cavity about ten inches deep and six inches in height and width will give a pair of bluebirds room for building a nest. The opening should not be more than two or two and one-half inches in diameter and there should be no threshold; this latter is a very particular point. If

Bluebirds often nest in man-made houses

there is a threshold or place to alight upon, the sparrows are likely to dispute with the bluebirds and drive them away, but the sparrow does not care for a place which has no threshold. The box for the bluebird may be made out of old boards or may be a section of an old tree trunk; it should be fastened from six to fifteen feet above the ground, and should be in nowise noticeable in color from its surroundings. To protect the nest from cats, barbed wire should be wound around the tree or post below the box. If the box for the nest is placed upon a post the barbed wire will also protect it from the squirrels. The eggs are bluish white; the young birds, in their first feathers, are spotted on the back and have whitish breasts mottled with brown. The food of the nestlings is almost entirely insects. In fact, this bird during its entire life is a great friend to man. The food of the adult is more than three-fourths insects and the remainder is wild berries and fruits, the winter food being largely mistletoe berries. It makes a specialty of injurious beetles, caterpillars and grasshoppers, and never touches any of our cultivated fruits. We should do everything in our power to encourage and protect these birds from their enemies, which are chiefly cats, squirrels and English sparrows.

The migration takes place in flocks during autumn, but it is done in a most leisurely manner with frequent stops where food is plenty. The bluebirds we see in September are probably not the ones we have had with us during the summer, but are those which have come from farther north.

They winter largely in the Gulf States; the writer has often heard them singing in midwinter in Southern Mississippi. The bluebirds seem to be the only ones that sing while at their winter resorts. They live the year round in the Bermudas, contrasting their heavenly blue plumage with the vivid red of the cardinals. The bluebird should not be confused with the indigo bunting; the latter is darker blue and has a blue breast.

References— Bulletin, Some Common Birds in Their Relation to Man, U. S. Dept. of Agr.; Bulletin, The Food of Nestling Birds, U. S. Dept. of Agr.; Birds in Their Relation to Man, Weed & Dearborn, pp. 86-88; Nature-Study and Life, Hodge, chapters 18-21; Junior Audubon Leaflets; Birds of Eastern North America, Chapman, 9. 403; Field Book of Wild Birds and Their Music, Mathews, pp. 251-254; Nature-Study in Elementary Schools, Wilson, p. 188.

> *"Winged lute that we call a bluebird,*
> *You blend in a silver strain*
> *The sound of the laughing waters,*
> *The patter of spring's sweet rain,*
> *The voice of the winds, the sunshine,*
> *And fragrance of blossoming things.*
> *Ah! You are an April poem,*
> *That God has dowered with wings."*
>
> —THE BLUEBIRD, REXFORD.

LESSON

Leading thought— The bluebird is related to the robins and thrushes and is as beneficial as it is beautiful. We should study its habits and learn how to make nesting boxes for it, and protect it in all ways.

Methods— The observations of this lesson must be made in the field and by the pupils individually. Give to each an outline of questions to answer through seeing. There should follow reading lessons on the bluebird's value to us and its winter migrations, and the lesson should end in discussions of best way to build boxes for its use in nesting season, its protection from cats and other enemies.

Observations—

1. Which comes North earlier in spring, the robin or the bluebird?

2. How do the two resemble each other and differ from each other?

3. Describe the bluebirds' song. Do they sing all summer?

4. Describe the colors of the bluebird as follows: The head, back, breast, under parts, wings, tail. How does the male bluebird differ from his mate in colors?

5. Where were the bluebirds you saw? What were they doing? If feeding, how did they act?

6. Can you see the color of the bluebird as plainly when it is in a tree as when it is flying? If not, why?

7. Where do the bluebirds build their nests? Of what material are the nests made? Do both parents work at the nest building?

8. What is the color of the eggs? How do the young birds look, when old enough to leave the nest, as compared with their parents?

9. What do the bluebirds eat? How do they benefit us? Do they do our fruit any injury?

10. What can we do to induce the bluebirds to live near our houses? How can we protect them?

11. Where do the bluebirds spend the winter?

12. Make a colored picture of a bluebird. How can we tell the bluebird from the indigo bunting?

13. What are the bluebirds' chief enemies?

Supplementary reading— *Nestlings of Forest and Marsh*, Wheelock, p. 62; *True Bird Stories*, Miller, p. 12; *How to Attract the Birds*, Blanchan; *Bird Neighbors*, Blanchan; *Our Birds and their Nestlings*, Walker, p. 17; *Familiar Wild Animals*, Lottridge; Audubon Leaflet, No. 24.

> *Hark! 'tis the bluebird's venturous strain*
> *High on the old fringed elm at the gate—*
> *Sweet-voiced, valiant on the swaying bough,*
> *Alert, elate,*
> *Dodging the fitful spits of snow,*
> *New England's poet-laureate*
> *Telling us Spring has come again!*
> —THOMAS BAILEY ALDRICH.

White Breasted Nuthatch

The White-Breasted Nuthatch

TEACHER'S STORY

"The busy nuthatch climbs his tree
Around the great bole spirally,
Peeping into wrinkles gray,
Under ruffled lichens gay,
Lazily piping one sharp note
From his silver mailèd throat."

—MAURICE THOMPSON.

BLITHE and mellow is the ringing "ank, ank" note of the nuthatch, and why need we allude to its nasal timbre! While it is not a strictly musical note, it has a most enticing quality and translates into sound the picture of bare-branched trees and the feeling of enchantment which permeates the forest in winter; it is one of the most "woodsy" notes in the bird repertoire. And while the singer of this note is not so bewitching as his constant chum the chickadee, yet it has many interesting ways quite its own. Nor is this "ank, ank," its only note.

A typical pose

I have often heard a pair talking to each other in sweet confidential syllables, "wit, wit, wit" very different from the loud note meant for the world at large. The nuthatches and chickadees hunt together all winter; it is no mere business partnership but a matter of congenial tastes. The chickadees hunt over the twigs and smaller branches, while the nuthatches usually prefer the tree trunks and the bases of the branches; both birds like the looks of the world upside down, and while the chickadee hangs head down from a twig, the nuthatch is quite likely to alight head down on a tree bole, holding itself safely in this position by thrusting its toes out at right angles to the body, thus getting a firm hold upon the bark. Sometimes its foot will be twisted completely around, the front toes pointed up the tree. The foot is well adapted for clinging to the bark as the front toes are strong and the hind toe is very long and is armed with a strong claw. Thus equipped, this bird runs about on the tree so rapidly, it has earned the name of "tree mouse". It often ascends a tree trunk spirally but is not so hidebound in this habit as is the brown creeper. It runs up or down freely head first and never flops down backwards like a woodpecker.

In color the nuthatch is bluish gray above with white throat and breast and reddish underparts. The sides of the head are white; the black cap extends back upon the neck but is not "pulled down" to the eyes like the chickadees. The wing feathers are dark brown edged with pale gray. The upper middle tail feathers are bluish like the back; the others are dark brown and tipped with white in such a manner that the tail when spread shows a broad white border on both sides. The most striking contrast between the chickadee and nuthatch in markings is that the latter lacks the black bib. However, its entire shape is very different from that of the chickadee and its beak is long and slender, being as long or longer than its head, while the beak of the chickadee is a short, sharp, little pick. The bill of the nuthatch is exactly fitted to reach in crevices of the bark and pull out hiding insects, or to hammer open the shell of nut or acorn and get both the meat of the nut and the grub feeding upon it. It will wedge an acorn into a seam in the bark and then throw back its head, woodpecker fashion, and drive home its chisel beak. But it does not always use common sense in this habit. I have often seen one cut off a piece of suet, fly off and thrust it into some crevice and hammer it as hard as if it were encased in a walnut shell. This always seems bad manners, like carrying off fruit from *table d'hote;* but the nuthatch is polite enough in using a napkin, for after eating the suet, it invariably wipes its bill on a branch, first one side then the other most assiduously until it is perfectly clean.

The nuthatches are a great benefit to our trees in winter, for then is when they hunt for hiding pests on their trunks. Their food consists of beetles, caterpillars, pupae of various insects, also seeds of ragweed, sunflowers, acorns, etc. While the nuthatch finds much of its food on trees, yet Mr. Torrey has seen it awkwardly turning over fallen leaves hunting for insects, and Mr. Baskett says it sometimes catches insects on the wing and gets quite out of breath from this unusual exercise.

It is only during the winter that we commonly see the nuthatches, for during the nesting season, they usually retire to the deep woods where they may occupy a cavity in a tree used by a woodpecker last year, or may make a hole for themselves with their sharp beaks. The nest is lined with leaves, feathers and hair; from five to nine creamy, speckled eggs are the treasure of this cave.

LESSON

Leading thought— The nuthatch is often a companion of the chickadees and woodpeckers. It has no black bib, like the chickadee, and it alights on a tree trunk head downward, which distinguishes it from woodpeckers.

Methods— This bird, like the chickadee and downy, gladly shares

The nuthatch runs head first down tree trunks in search of insects

the suet banquet we prepare for them and may be observed at leisure while "at table." The contrast between the habits of the nuthatch and those of its companions make it a most valuable aid in stimulating close and keen observation on the part of the pupils.

Observations—

1. Where have you seen the nuthatches? Were they with other birds? What other birds?

2. Does a nuthatch usually alight on the ends of the branches of a tree or on the trunk and larger limbs? Does it usually alight head down or up? When it runs down the tree, does it go head first or does it back down? When it ascends the tree does it follow a spiral path? Does it use its tail for a brace when climbing, as does the downy?

3. How are the nuthatch's toes arranged to assist it in climbing? Are the three front toes of each foot directed downward when the bird alights head downward? How does it manage its feet when in this position?

4. What is the general color of the nuthatch above and below? The color of the top and sides of head? Color of back? Wings? Tail? Throat?

Breast?

5. Does the black cap come down to the eyes on the nuthatch as on the chickadee? Has the nuthatch a black bib?

6. What is the shape of the beak of the nuthatch? For what is it adapted? How does it differ from the beak of the chickadee?

7. What is the food of the nuthatch? Where is it found? Does it open nuts for the grubs or the nut meat? Observe the way it strikes its beak into the suet. Why does it strike so hard?

8. How would you spell this bird's note? Have you heard it give more than one note?

9. How does the nuthatch benefit our trees? At what season does it benefit them most? Why?

10. Where do the nuthatches build their nests? Why do we see the nuthatches oftener in winter than in summer?

Black-capped chickadee

The Chickadee

"He is the hero of the woods; there are courage and good nature enough in that compact little body, which you may hide in your fist, to supply a whole groveful of May songsters. He has the Spartan virtue of an eagle, the cheerfulness of a thrush, the nimbleness of Cock Sparrow, the endurance of the seabirds condensed into his tiny frame, and there have been added a pertness and ingenuity all his own. His curiosity is immense, and his audacity equal to it; I have even had one alight upon the barrel of the gun over my shoulders as I sat quietly under his tree."

—ERNEST INGERSOLL.

HOWEVER careless we may be of our bird friends when we are in the midst of the luxurious life of summer, even the most careless among us give pleased attention to the birds that bravely endure with us the rigors of winter. And when this winged companion of winter proves to be the most fascinating little ball of feathers ever created, constantly overflowing with cheerful song, our pleased attention changes to active delight. Thus it is, that in all the lands of snowy winters the chickadee is a loved comrade of the country wayfarer; that happy song "chick-a-dee-dee-dee" finds its way to the dullest consciousness and the most callous heart.

The chickadees appear in small flocks in the winter and often in company with the nuthatches. The chickadees work on the twigs and ends of branches, while the nuthatches usually mine the bark of the trunk and larger branches, the former hunting insect eggs and the latter, insects tucked away in winter quarters. When the chickadee is prospecting for eggs, it looks the twig over, first above and then hangs head down and inspects it from below; it is a thorough worker and doesn't intend to overlook anything whatever; and however busily it is hunting, it always finds time for singing; whether on the wing or perched upon a twig or hanging from it like an acrobat, head down, it sends forth its happy "chickadeedee" to assure us that this world is all right and good enough for anybody. Besides this song, it begins in February to sing a most seductive "fee-bee," giving a rising inflection to the first syllable and a long, falling inflection to the last, which makes it a very different song from the short, jerky notes of the phoebe-bird, which cuts the last syllable short and gives it a rising inflection. More than this, the chickadee has some chatty conversational notes, and now and then performs a bewitching little yodle, which is a fit expression of its own delicious personality.

The general effect of the colors of the chickadee is grayish brown above and grayish white below. The top of the head is black, the sides white, and it has a seductive little black bib under its chin. The back is grayish, the wings and tail are dark gray, the feathers having white margins. The breast is grayish white changing to buff or brownish at the sides and below. It is often called the "Black-capped Titmouse," and it may always be distinguished by black cap and black bib. It is smaller than the English sparrow; its beak is a sharp little pick just fitted for taking insect eggs off twigs and from under bark. Insects are obliged to pass the winter in some stage of their existence, and many of them wisely remain in the egg until there is something worth doing in the way of eating. These eggs are glued fast to the food trees by the mother insect and thus provides abundant food for the chickadees.

It has been estimated that one chickadee will destroy several hundred insect eggs in one day, and it has been proven that orchards frequented by these birds are much more free from insect pests than other orchards in the same locality. They can be enticed into orchards by putting up beef fat or bones and thus we can secure their valuable service. In summer these birds attack caterpillars and other insects.

When it comes to nest building, if the chickadees cannot find a house to rent they proceed to dig out a proper hole from some decaying tree, which they line with moss, feathers, fur or some other soft material. The nest is often not higher than six to ten feet from the ground. One which I studied was in a decaying fence post. The eggs are white, sparsely speckled and spotted with lilac or rufous. The young birds are often eight in number and how these fubsy birdlings manage to pack themselves in such a small hole is a wonder, and probably gives them good discipline in bearing hardships cheerfully.

Reference— Useful Birds and Their Protection, Forbush, p. 163; Birds of Village and Field, Merriam; Bird Neighbors, Blanchan.

TONYCASTRO (CC BY 4.0)

Chestnut-backed Chickadee

LESSON

Leading thought— The chickadee is as useful as it is delightful; it remains in the North during winter, working hard to clear our trees of insect eggs and singing cheerily all day. It is so friendly that we can induce it to come even to the window sill, by putting out suet to show our friendly interest.

Methods— Put beef fat on the trees near the schoolhouse in December and replenish it afresh about every two or three weeks. The chickadees will come to the feast and may be observed all winter. Give the questions a few at a time and let the children read in the bird books a record of the benefits derived from this bird.

Observations—

1. Where have you seen the chickadees? What were they doing? Were there several together?

2. What is the common song of the chickadee? What other notes has it? Have you heard it yodle? Have you heard it sing "fe-bee, fee-bee"? How does this song differ from that of the phoebe-bird? Does it sing on the wing or when at rest?

3. What is the color of the chickadee: Top and sides of head, back, wings, tail, throat, breast, under parts? Compare size of chickadee with that of English sparrow.

4. What is the shape of the chickadee's bill and for what is it adapted? What is the food in winter? Where does the bird find it? How does it act when feeding and hunting for food?

5. Does the chickadee usually alight on the ends of the branches or on the larger portions near the trunk of the tree?

6. How can you distinguish the chickadees from their companions, the nuthatches?

7. Does the chickadee ever seem discouraged by the snow and cold weather? Do you know another name for the chickadee?

8. Where does it build its nest? Of what material? Have you ever watched one of these nests? If so, tell about it.

9. How does the chickadee benefit our orchards and shade trees? How can we induce it to feel at home with us and work for us?

Supplementary reading— "Foster Baby," *Nestlings of Forest and Marsh*; "Ch'-geegee-lokh-sis," *Ways of Wood Folk*; "Why a Chickadee Goes Crazy," *Animal Heroes*, Seton; "The Titmouse," a poem, by Emerson.

The Downy Woodpecker

FRIEND DOWNY is the name this attractive little neighbor has earned, because it is so friendly to those of us who love trees. Watch it as it hunts each crack and crevice of the bark of your favorite apple or shade tree, seeking assiduously for cocoons and insects hiding there, and you will soon, of your own accord, call it friend; you will soon love its black and white uniform, which consists of a black coat speckled and barred with white and whitish gray vest and trousers. The front of the head is black and there is a black streak extending backward from the eye with a white streak above and also below it. The male has a vivid red patch on the back of the head, but his wife shows no such giddiness; plain black and white are good enough for her. In both sexes the throat and breast are white, the middle tail feathers black, while the side tail feathers are white, barred with black at their tips.

The downy has a way of alighting low down on a tree trunk or at the base of a larger branch and climbing upward in a jerky fashion; it never runs about over the tree nor does it turn around and go down head first, like the nuthatch; if it wishes to go down a short distance it accomplishes this by a few awkward, backward hops; but when it really wishes to descend, it flies off and down. The downy, as other woodpeckers, has a special arrangement of its physical machinery to enable it to climb trees in its own manner. In order to grasp the bark on the side of the tree more firmly, its fourth toe is turned backward to work as companion with the thumb. Thus it is able to clutch the bark as with a pair of nippers, two claws in front and two claws behind; and as another aid, the tail is arranged to prop the bird, like a bracket. The tail is rounded in shape and the middle feathers have rather strong quills; but the secret of the adhesion of the tail to the bark lies in the great profusion of barbs which, at the edge of the feathers, offer bristling tips, and when applied to the side of the tree act like a wire brush with all the wires pushing downward. This explains why the woodpecker cannot go backward without lifting the tail.

But even more wonderful than this, is the mechanism by which the downy and hairy woodpeckers get their food, which consists largely of wood-borers or larvae working under the bark. When the woodpecker wishes to get a grub in the wood, it seizes the bark firmly with its feet, uses

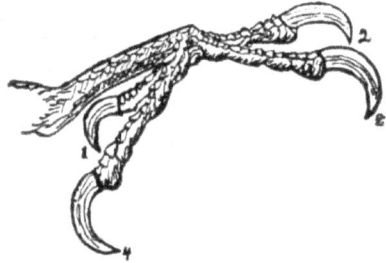

Friend Downy's foot.

its tail as a brace, throws its head and upper part of the body as far back as possible, and then drives a powerful blow with its strong beak. The beak is adapted for just this purpose, as it is wedge-shaped at the end, and is used like a mason's drill sometimes, and sometimes like a pick. When the bird uses its beak as a pick, it strikes hard, deliberate blows and the chips fly; but when it is drilling, it strikes rapidly and not so hard and quickly drills a small, deep hole leading directly to the burrow of the grub. When finally the grub is reached, it would seem well nigh impossible to pull it out through a hole which is too small and deep to admit of the beak being used as pincers. This is another story and a very interesting one; the downy and hairy can both extend their tongues far beyond the point of the beak, and the tip of the tongue is hard and horny and covered with short backward-slanting hooks acting like a spear or harpoon, and when thrust into the grub pulls it out easily (see initial). The bones of the tongue have a spring arrangement; when not in use, the tongue lies soft in the mouth, like a wrinkled earthworm, but when in use, the bones spring out, stretching it to its full length and it is then slim and small. The process is like fastening a pencil to the tip of a glove finger; when drawn back the finger is wrinkled together, but when thrust out, straightens. This spring arrangement of the bones of the woodpecker's tongue is a marvellous mechanism and should be studied through pictures; see Birds, Eckstrom, Chapter XIV; The Bird, Beebe, p. 122; "The Tongues of Woodpeckers," Lucas, U. S. Department of Agriculture.

Since the food of the downy and the hairy is where they can get it all winter, there is no need for them to go South; thus they stay with us and work for us the entire year. We should try to make them feel at home with us in our orchards and shade trees by putting up pieces of beef fat, to convince them of their welcome. No amount of free food will pauperize these birds, for as soon as they have eaten of the fat, they commence to hunt for grubs on the tree and thus earn their feast. They never injure live wood.

James Whitcomb Riley describes the drumming of the woodpecker as "weeding out the lonesomeness" and that is exactly what the drumming of the woodpecker means. The male selects some dried limb of hard wood and there beats out his well-known signal which advertises far and near, "Wanted, a wife." And after he wins her, he still drums on for a time to cheer her while she is busy with her family cares. The woodpecker has no voice for singing, like the robin or thrush; and luckily, he does not insist on singing, like the peacock whether he can or not. He chooses rather to devote his voice to terse and business-like conversation; and when he is musically inclined, he turns drummer. He is rather particular about his instrument and having found one that is sufficiently resonant he returns to it day after day. While it is ordinarily the male that drums I once observed a female drumming. I told her that she was a bold minx and ought to be ashamed of herself; but within twenty minutes she had drummed up two red-capped suitors who chased each other about with great animosity, so her performance was evidently not considered improper in woodpecker society. I have watched a rival pair of male downies fight for hours at a time,

Downy woodpeckers looking to build a nest

but their duel was of the French brand,—much fuss and no bloodshed. They advanced upon each other with much haughty glaring and scornful bobs of the head, but when they were sufficiently near to stab each other they beat a mutual and circumspect retreat. Although we hear the male downies drumming every spring, I doubt if they are calling for new wives; I believe they are, instead, calling the attention of their lawful spouses to the fact that it is time for nest building to begin. I have come to this conclusion because the downies and hairies which I have watched for years have always come in pairs to partake of suet during the entire winter; and while only one at a time sits at meat and the lord and master is somewhat bossy, yet they seem to get along as well as most married pairs.

The downy's nest is a hole, usually in a partly decayed tree; an old apple tree is a favorite site and a fresh excavation is made each year. There are from four to six white eggs, which are laid on a nice bed of chips as fine almost as sawdust. The door to the nest is a perfect circle and about an inch and a quarter across.

The hairy woodpecker is fully one-third larger than the downy, measuring nine inches from tip of beak to tip of tail, while the downy measures only about six inches. The tail feathers at the side are white for the entire length, while they are barred at the tips in the downy. There is a black "parting" through the middle of the red patch on the back of the hairy's head. The two species are so much alike that it is difficult for the beginner to tell them apart. Their habits are very similar, except that the hairy lives in the woods and is not so commonly seen in orchards or on shade trees. The food of the hairy is much like that of the downy and it is, therefore, a beneficial bird and should be protected.

Cross-section of a tree showing a downy woodpecker nest

LESSON

Leading thought— The downy woodpecker remains with us all winter, feeding upon insects that are wintering in crevices and beneath the bark of our trees. It is fitted especially by shape of beak, tongue, feet and tail to get such food and it is a "friend in need" to our forest, shade and orchard trees.

Methods— If a piece of beef fat be fastened upon the trunk or branch of a tree, which can be seen from the schoolroom windows, there will be no lack of interest in this friendly little bird; for the downy will sooner or later find this feast spread for it and will come every day to partake. Give out the questions, a few at a time, and discuss the answers with the pupils.

Observations—

1. What is the general color of the downy above and below? The color of the top of the head? Sides of the head? The throat and breast? The color and markings of the wings? Color and markings of the middle and side tail-feathers?

2. Do all downy woodpeckers have the red patch at the back of the head? If not, why?

3. What is the note of the downy? Does it make any other sound? Have you ever seen one drumming? At what time of the year? On what did it drum? What did it use for a drumstick? What do you suppose was the purpose of this music?

4. How does the downy climb a tree trunk? How does it descend? How do its actions differ from those of the nuthatch?

5. How are the woodpecker's toes arranged to help it climb a tree trunk? How does this arrangement of toes differ from that of other birds?

6. How does the downy use its tail to assist it in climbing? What is the shape of the tail and how is it adapted to assist?

7. What does the downy eat and where does it find its food? Describe how it gets at its food. What is the shape of its bill and how is it fitted for getting the food? Tell how the downy's tongue is used to spear the grub.

8. Why does the downy not go South in winter?

9. Of what use is this bird to us? How should we protect it and entice it into our orchards?

10. Write an English theme on the subject "How the downy builds its nest and rears its young".

Supplementary reading— *The Woodpeckers,* Eckstorm; *Bird Neighbors,* Blanchan; *Winter Neighbors,* Burroughs.

A few seasons ago a downy woodpecker, probably the individual one who is now my winter neighbor, began to drum early in March in a partly decayed apple-tree that stands in the edge of a narrow strip of woodland near me. When the morning was still and mild I would often hear him through my window before I was up, or by half-past six o'clock, and he would keep it up pretty briskly till nine or ten o'clock, in this respect resembling the grouse, which do most of their drumming in the forenoon. His drum was the stub of a dry limb about the size of one's wrist. The heart was decayed and gone, but the outer shell was loud and resonant. The bird would keep his position there for an hour at a time. Between his drummings he would preen his plumage and listen as if for the response of the female, or for the drum of some rival. How swift his head would go when he was delivering his blows upon the limb! His beak wore the surface perceptibly. When he wished to change the key, which was quite often, he would shift his position an inch or two to a knot which gave out a higher, shriller note. When I climbed up to examine his drum he was much disturbed. I did not know he was in the vicinity, but it seems he saw me from a near tree, and came in haste to the neighboring branches, and with spread plumage and a sharp note demanded plainly enough what my business was with his drum. I was invading his privacy, desecrating his shrine, and the bird was much put out. After some weeks the female appeared, he had literally drummed up a mate; his urgent and oft-repeated advertisement was answered. Still the drumming did not cease, but was quite as fervent as before. If a mate could be won by drumming she could be kept and entertained by more drumming; courtship should not end with marriage. If the bird felt musical before, of course he felt much more so now. Besides that, the gentle deities needed propitiating in behalf of the nest and young as well as in behalf of the mate. After a time a second female came, when there was war between the two. I did not see them come to blows, but I saw one female pursuing the other about the place, and giving her no rest for several days. She was evidently trying to run her out of the neighborhood. Now and then she, too, would drum briefly as if sending a triumphant message to her mate.

—Winter Neighbors, John Burroughs.

The yellow-bellied sapsucker

The Sapsucker

TEACHER'S STORY

THE sapsucker is a woodpecker that has strayed from the paths of virtue; he has fallen into temptation by the wayside, and instead of drilling a hole for the sake of the grub at the end of it, he drills for drink. He is a tippler, and sap is his beverage; and he is also fond of the soft, inner bark. He often drills his holes in regular rows and thus girdles a limb or a tree, and for this is pronounced a rascal by men who have themselves ruthlessly cut from our land millions of trees that should now be standing. It is amusing to see a sapsucker take his tipple, unless his saloon happens to be one of our prized young trees. He uses his bill as a pick and makes the chips fly as he taps the tree; then he goes away and taps another tree. After a time he comes back and, holding his beak close to the hole for a long time, seems to be sucking up the sap; he then throws back his head and "swigs" it down with every sign of delirious enjoyment. The avidity with which these birds come to the bleeding wells which they have made, has in it all the fierceness of a toper crazy for drink; they are particularly fond of the sap of the mountain ash, apple, thorn apple, canoe birch, cut-leaf

93

LOTUSGREEN (CC BY 4.0)

*The patterns left in the bark of a Chinese Evergreen Elm
after repeated visits by a Yellow-Bellied Sapsucker*

birch, red maple, red oak, white ash and young pines. However, the sapsucker does not live solely on sap, he also feeds upon insects whenever he can find them. When feeding their young, the sapsuckers are true flycatchers, snatching insects while on the wing. The male has the crown and throat crimson, edged with black with a black line extending back of the eye, bordered with white above and below. There is a large, black circular patch on the breast which is bordered at the sides and below with lemon yellow. The female is similar to the male and has a red forehead, but she has a white bib instead of a red one beneath the chin. The distinguishing marks of the sapsucker should be learned by the pupils. The red is on the front of the head instead of on the crown, as is the case with the downy and hairy; when it is flying the broad, white stripes extending from the shoulders backward, form a long, oval figure, which is very characteristic.

The sapsuckers spend the winter in the Southern States where they drill wells in the white oak and other trees. From Virginia to Northern New York and New England, where they breed, they are seen only during migration, which occurs in April; then the birds appear two and three together and are very bold in attacking shade trees, especially the white birch. They nest only in the Northern United States and northward. The nest is usually a hole in a tree about forty feet from the ground, and is likely to be in a dead birch.

LESSON

Leading thought— The sapsucker has a red cap, a red bib and a yellow breast; it is our only woodpecker that does injury to trees. We should learn to distinguish it from the downy and hairy, as the latter are among the best bird friends of the trees.

Methods— Let the observations begin with the study of the trees which have been attacked by the sapsucker, which are almost everywhere common, and thus lead to an interest in the culprit.

Observations—

1. Have you seen the work of the sapsucker? Are the holes drilled in rows completely around the tree? If there are two rows or more, are the holes set evenly one below another?

2. Do the holes sink into the wood, or are they simply through the bark? Why does it injure or kill a tree to be girdled with these holes? Have you ever seen the sapsuckers making these holes? If so, how did they act?

3. How many kinds of trees can you find punctured by these holes? Are they likely to be young trees?

4. How can you distinguish the sapsucker from the other woodpeckers? How have the hairy and downy, which are such good friends of the trees, been made to suffer for the sapsucker's sins?

5. What is the color of the sapsucker as follows: Forehead, sides of head, back, wings, throat, upper and lower breast? What is the difference in color between the male and female?

6. In what part of the country do the sapsuckers build their nests? Where do they make their nests and how?

Supplementary reading— *Bird Neighbors*, Blanchan; *Birds, Bees and Sharp Eyes*, John Burroughs.

In the following winter the same bird (a sapsucker) tapped a maple-tree in front of my window in fifty-six places; and, when the day was sunny and the sap oozed out he spent most of his time there. He knew the good sap-days, and was on hand promptly for his tipple; cold and cloudy days he did not appear. He knew which side of the tree to tap, too, and avoided the sunless northern exposure. When one series of well-holes failed to supply him, he would sink another, drilling through the bark with great ease and quickness. Then, when the day was warm, and the sap ran freely, he would have a regular sugar-maple debauch, sitting there by his wells hour after hour, and as fast as they became filled sipping out the sap. This he did in a gentle, caressing manner that was very suggestive. He made a row of wells near the foot of the tree, and other rows higher up, and he would hop up and down the trunk as they became filled.

—WINTER NEIGHBORS, JOHN BURROUGHS.

Having a drink

The Red-Headed Woodpecker

THE red-head is well named, for his helmet and visor show a vivid glowing crimson that stirs the sensibilities of the color lover. It is readily distinguished from the other woodpeckers because its entire head and bib are red. For the rest, it is a beautiful dark metallic blue with the lower back, a band across the wing, and the under parts white; its outer tail feathers are tipped with white. The female is colored like the male, but the young have the head and breast gray, streaked with black and white, and the wings barred with black. It may make its nest by excavating a hole in a tree or a stump or even in a telegraph pole; the eggs are glossy white. This woodpecker is quite different in habits from the hairy and downy, as it likes to flit along from stump to fence-post and catch insects on the wing, like a fly-catcher. The only time that it pecks wood is when it is making a hole for its nest.

As a drummer, the red-head is most adept and his roll is a long one. He is an adaptable fellow, and if there is no resonant dead limb at hand, he has been known to drum on tin roofs and lightning rods; and once we also observed him executing a most brilliant solo on the wire of a barbed fence. He is especially fond of beechnuts and acorns, and being a thrifty fellow as well as musical, in time of plenty he stores up food against time of need. He places his nuts in crevices and forks of the branches or in holes in trees or any other hiding place. He can shell a beechnut quite as cleverly as can the deer mouse; and he is own cousin to the Carpenter Woodpecker of the Pacific Coast, which is also red-headed and which drills holes in the oak trees wherein he drives acorns like pegs for later use.

LESSON

Leading thought— The red-headed woodpecker has very different habits from the downy and is not so useful to us. It lives upon nuts and fruit and such insects as it can catch upon the wing.

Methods— If there is a red-head in the vicinity of your school the children will be sure to see it. Write the following questions upon the blackboard and offer a prize to the first one who will make a note on where the red-head stores his winter food.

Observations—

1. Can you tell the red-head from the other woodpeckers? What colors especially mark his plumage?

2. Where does the red-head nest? Describe eggs and nest.

3. What have you observed the red-head eating? Have you noticed it storing nuts and acorns for the winter? Have you noticed it flying off with cherries or other fruit?

4. What is the note of the red-head? Have you ever seen one drumming? What did he use for a drum? Did he come back often to this place to make his music?

Supplementary reading— "The House That Fell" in *Nestlings of Forest and Marsh*; *Our Birds and their Nestlings*, p. 90; *Birds, Bees and Sharp Eyes*, John Burroughs.

Another trait our woodpeckers have that endears them to me, and that has never been pointedly noticed by our ornithologists, is their habit of drumming in the spring. They are songless birds, and yet all are musicians; they make the dry limbs eloquent of the coming change. Did you think that loud, sonorous hammering which proceeded from the orchard or from the near woods on that still March or April morning was only some bird getting its breakfast? It is downy, but he is not rapping at the door of a grub; he is rapping at the door of spring, and the dry limb thrills beneath the ardor of his blows. Or, later in the season, in the dense forest or by some remote mountain lake, does that measured rhythmic beat that breaks upon the silence, first three strokes following each other rapidly, succeeded by two louder ones with longer intervals between them, and that has an effect upon the alert ear as if the solitude itself had at least found a voice—does that suggest anything less than a deliberate musical performance? In fact, our woodpeckers are just as characteristically drummers as is the ruffed grouse, and they have their particular limbs and stubs to which they resort for that purpose. Their need of expression is apparently just as great as that of the song-birds, and it is not surprising that they should have found out that there is music in a dry, seasoned limb which can be evoked beneath their beaks.

The woodpeckers do not each have a particular dry limb to which they resort at all times to drum, like the one I have described. The woods are full of suitable branches, and they drum more or less here and there as they are in quest of food; yet I am convinced each one has its favorite spot, like the grouse, to which it resorts, especially in the morning. The sugar-maker in the maple woods may notice that this sound proceeds from the same tree or trees about his camp with great regularity. A woodpecker in my vicinity has drummed for two seasons on a telegraph-pole, and he makes the wires and glass insulators ring. Another drums on a thin board on the end of a long grape-arbor, and on still mornings can be heard a long distance.

A friend of mine in a Southern city tells me of a red-headed woodpecker that drums upon a lightning-rod on his neighbor's house. Nearly every clear, still morning at certain seasons, he says, this musical rapping may be heard. "He alternates his tapping with his stridulous call, and the effect on a cool, autumn-like morning is very pleasing."
—Birds, Bees and Sharp Eyes, John Burroughs.

A northern flicker

The Flicker or Yellow-Hammer

TEACHER'S STORY

THE first time I ever saw a flicker I said, "What a wonderful mead-ow-lark and what is it doing on that ant hill?" But, another glance re-vealed to me a red spot on the back of the bird's neck, and as soon as I was sure that it was not a bloody gash, I knew that it marked no meadow-lark. The top of the flicker's head and its back are slaty-gray, which is much enlivened by a bright red band across the nape of the neck. The tail is black above and yellow tipped with black below; the wings are black, but have a beautiful luminous yellow beneath, which is very noticeable during flight. There is a locket adorning the breast which is a thin, black crescent, much narrower than that of the mead-ow-lark. Below the locket, the breast is yellowish white thickly marked with circular, black spots. The throat and sides of the head are pinkish brown, and the male has a black mustache extending backward from

100

the beak with a very fashionable droop. Naturally enough the female, although she resembles her spouse, lacks his mustache. The beak is long, strong, somewhat curved and dark colored. This bird is distinctly larger than the robin. The white patch on the rump shows little or none when the bird is at rest, for this white mark is a "color call," it being a rear signal by means of which the flock of migrating birds are able to keep together in the night. The yellow-hammer's flight is wave-like and jerky and quite different from that of the meadow-lark; nor does it stay so constantly in the meadows but often frequents woods and orchards.

The flicker has many names, such as golden-winged woodpecker, yellow-hammer, high-hole, yarup, wake-up, clape and many others. It earned the name of high-hole because of its habit of excavating its nest high up in trees, usually between ten and twenty-five feet from the ground. It especially loves an old apple tree as a site for a nest, and most of our large old orchards can boast of a pair of these handsome birds during the nesting season of May and June. The flicker is not above renting any house he finds vacant, excavated by some other birds last year. He earned his name of yarup or wake-up from his spring song, which is a rollicking, jolly "wick-a, wick-a, wick-a-wick," a song commonly heard the last of March or early April. The chief food of the flicker is ants, although it also eats beetles, flies and wild fruit, but does little or no damage to planted crops. So long has it fed upon ants, that its tongue has become modified, like that of the ant-eater; it is covered with a sticky substance; and when it is thrust into an ant hill, all of the little citizens, disturbed in their communal labors, at once bravely attack the intruder and become glued fast to it, and are thus withdrawn and transferred to the capacious stomach of the bird. It has been known to eat three thousand ants at a single meal.

Those who have observed the flicker during the courting season declare him to be the most silly and vain of all bird wooers. Mr. Baskett says: "When he wishes to charm his sweetheart he mounts a small twig near her, and lifts his wings, spreads his tail, and begins to nod right and left as he exhibits his mustache to his charmer. He sets his jet locket first on one side of the twig and then on the other. He may even go so far as to turn his head half around to show her the pretty

The male flicker has a black mustache

spot on his back hair. In doing all this he performs the most ludicrous antics and has the silliest expression of face and voice as if in losing his heart, as some one phrases it, he had lost his head also."

The nest hole is quite deep and the white eggs are from four to ten in number. The feeding of the young flickers is a painful process to watch. The parent takes the food into its own stomach and partially digests it, then thrusting its own bill down the throat of the young one it pumps the soft food into it "kerchug, kerchug," until it seems as if the young one must be shaken to its foundations. The young flickers, as soon as they leave the nest, climb around freely on the home tree in a delightful, playful manner.

LESSON

Leading thought— The flicker is a true woodpecker but has changed its habits and spends much of its time in meadows hunting for ants and other insects; it makes its nest in trees, like its relatives. It can be distinguished from the meadow-lark by the white patch above the tail which shows during flight.

Methods— This is one of the most important of birds of the meadow and the work may be done in September when there are plenty of young flickers, which have not learned to be wary. The observations

102

A female yellow-shafted northern flicker

may be made in the field, a few questions given at a time.

Observations—

1. Where do you find the flicker in the summer and early autumn? How can you tell it from the meadow-lark in color and in flight?

2. What is it doing in the meadows? How does it manage to trap ants?

3. What is the size of the flicker as compared to the robin? What is its general color as compared to the meadow-lark?

4. Describe the colors of the flicker as follows: Top and sides of the head, back of the neck, lower back, tail, wings, throat and breast. The color and shape of the beak. Is there a difference in markings between the males and females?

5. Does the patch of white above the tail show, except when the bird is flying? Of what use is this to the bird?

6. What is the flicker's note? At what time of spring do you hear it first?

7. Where does the flicker build its nest and how? What is the color of the eggs? How many are there?

8. How does it feed its young? How do the young flickers act?

9. How many names do you know for the flicker?

Supplementary reading— "The Bird of Many Names," *Nestlings of Forest and Marsh*; *A Fellow of Expedients*, Long; *Our Birds and Their Nestlings*, p. 187; Audubon Leaflet No. 5.

The high-hole appears to drum more promiscuously than does the downy. He utters his long, loud spring call, whick-whick-whick, and then begins to rap with his beak upon his perch before the last note has reached your ear. I have seen him drum sitting upon the ridge of the barn. The log-cock, or pileated woodpecker, the largest and wildest of our Northern species, I have never heard drum. His blows should wake the echoes.

When the woodpecker is searching for food, or laying siege to some hidden grub, the sound of his hammering is dead or muffled, and is heard but a few yards. It is only upon dry, seasoned timber, freed of its bark, that he beats his reveille to spring and woos his mate.

—Birds, Bees and Sharp Eyes, John Burroughs.

Western meadowlark

The Meadow-Lark

TEACHER'S STORY

THE first intimation we have in early spring, that the meadow-lark is again with us, comes to us through his soft, sweet, sad note which Van Dyke describes so graphically when he says it "leaks slowly upward from the ground." One wonders how a bird can express happiness in these melancholy, sweet, slurred notes and yet undoubtedly it is a song expressing joy, the joy of returning home, the happiness of love and of nest building. But after one has spent a winter in the Gulf States, and has witnessed the slaughter there of this most valuable bird; and after the northern stomach and heart have turned sick at the sight of breasts once so full of song done brown on the luncheon table, one no longer wonders that the meadow-lark's song of joy is fraught with sadness. There should be national laws to protect the birds that are of value to one part of the United States from being slaughtered in their winter haunts, unless they are there a nuisance and injurious to crops, which is not the case with the meadow-lark.

A western Meadowlark nest in native prairie

The meadow-lark, as is indicated by its name, is a bird of the meadow. It is often confused with another bird of the meadow which has very different habits, the flicker. The two are approximately of the same size and color and each has a black crescent or locket on the breast and each shows the "white feather" during flight. The latter is the chief distinguishing character; the outer tail feathers of the mead-ow-lark are white, while the tail feathers of the flicker are not white at all, but it has a single patch of white on the rump. The flight of the two is quite different. The lark lifts itself by several sharp movements and then soars smoothly over the course, while the flicker makes a contin-uous up and down, wave-like flight. The songs of the two would surely never be confused, for the meadow-lark is among our sweetest sing-ers, to which class the flicker with his "flick a flick" hardly belongs.

The colors of the meadow-lark are most harmonious shades of brown and yellow, well set off by the black locket on its breast. Its wings are light brown, each feather being streaked with black and brown; the line above the eye is yellow, bordered with black above and below; a buff line extends from the beak backward over the crown. The wings are light brown and have a mere suggestion of white bars; portions of the outer feathers on each side of the tail are white, but this white does not show except during flight. The sides of the throat are greenish, the middle part and breast are lemon-yellow, with the large, black crescent just below the throat. The beak is long, strong and black, and the meadow-lark is decidedly a low-browed bird, the forehead being only slightly higher than the upper part of the beak. It is a little larger than the robin which it rivals in plumpness.

The meadow-lark has a particular liking for meadows which border streams. It sings when on the ground, on the bush or fence and while on the wing; and it sings during the entire period of its northern stay, from April to November, except while it is moulting in late summer. Mr. Mathews, who is an eminent authority on bird songs, says that the meadow-larks of New York have a different song from those of Vermont or Nantucket, although the music has always the same general characteristics. The western species has a longer and more complex song than ours of the East. It is one of the few California birds that is a genuine joy to the eastern visitor; during February and March its heavenly music is as pervasive as the California sunshine.

The nest is built in a depression in the ground near a tuft of grass; it is constructed of coarse grass and sticks and is lined with finer grass; there is usually a dome of grass blades woven above the nest; and often a long, covered vestibule leading to the nest is made in a similar fashion. This is evidently for protection from the keen eyes of hawks and crows. The eggs are laid about the last of May and are usually from five to seven in number; they are white, speckled with brown and purple. The young larks are usually large enough to be out of the way before haying time in July.

The food of the meadow-lark during the entire year consists almost exclusively of insects which destroy the grass of our meadows. It eats great quantities of grasshoppers, cut worms, chinch bugs, army worms, wire worms, weevils, and also destroys some weed seeds. Each pupil should make a diagram in his note-book showing the proportions of the meadow-lark's different kinds of food. This may be copied from Audubon Leaflet No. 3. The killing of the meadow-lark in New York State is a punishable offence, as it should be in every state of the Union. Everyone who owns a meadow should use his influence to the uttermost to protect this valuable bird. It has been estimated that the meadow-larks save, to every township where hay is produced, twenty-five dollars each year on this crop alone.

LESSON

Leading thought— The meadow-lark is of great value in delivering the grass of our meadows from insect destroyers. It has a song which we all know; it can be identified by color as a large, light brown bird with white feathers on each side of the tail, and in flight, by its quick up and down movements finishing with long, low, smooth sailing.

Method— September and October are good months for observations on the flight, song and appearance of the meadow-lark, and also for learning how to distinguish it

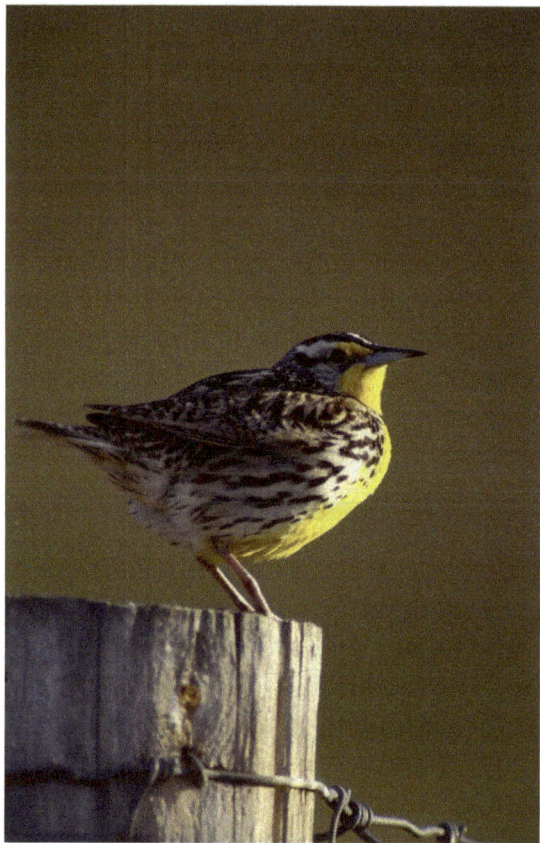
Western meadowlark

from the flicker. The notes must be made by the pupils in the field, and after they know the bird and its song let them, if they have opportunity, study the bird books and bulletins, and prepare written accounts of the way the meadow-lark builds its nest and of its economic value.

Observations—

1. Where have you seen the meadow-lark? Did you ever see it in the woods? Describe its flight. How can you identify it by color when it is flying? How do its white patches and its flight differ from those of the flicker?

2. Try and imitate the meadow-lark's notes by song or whistle. Does it sing while on the ground, or on a bush or fence, or during flight?

3. Note the day when you hear its last song in the fall and also its first song in the spring. Does it sing during August and September?

Why? Where does it spend the winter? On what does it feed while in the South? How are our meadow-larks treated when on their southern sojourn?

4. Is the meadow-lark larger or smaller than the robin? Describe from your own observation, as far as possible, the colors of the meadow-lark as follows: Top of head; line above the eye; back; wings; tail; throat; breast; locket; color and shape of beak. Make a sketch of your own or a copy from Louis Fuertes' excellent picture of the meadow-lark in the Audubon Leaflet, and color it accurately.

5. When is the nest built; where is it placed; of what material is it built? How is it protected from sight from above? Why this protection? How many eggs? What are their colors and markings?

6. What is the food of the meadow-lark? Copy the diagram from the Audubon leaflet, showing the proportions of the different kinds of insects which it destroys. Why should the farmers of the South also protect the meadow-lark by law?

Supplementary reading—Audubon Education Leaflet No. 3; Farmers' Bulletin No. 54, U. S. Dept. of Agr.; "A Pioneer," in *Nestlings of Forest and Marsh,* Wheelock.

> *Sweet, sweet, sweet! O happy that I am!*
> *(Listen to the meadow-larks, across the fields that sing!)*
> *Sweet, sweet, sweet! O subtle breath of balm,*
> *O winds that blow, O buds that grow, O rapture of the spring!*
> *Sweet, sweet, sweet! O happy world that is!*
> *Dear heart, I hear across the fields my mateling pipe and call.*
> *Sweet, sweet, sweet! O world so full of bliss,*
> *For life is love, the world is love, and love is over all!*
> —INA COOLBRITH.

A pair of sparrows

The English Sparrow

TEACHER'S STORY

So dainty in plumage and hue,
A study in grey and in brown,
How little, how little we knew
The pest he would prove to the town!
From dawn until daylight grows dim,
Perpetual chatter and scold.
No winter migration for him,
Not even afraid of the cold!
Scarce a song-bird he fails to molest,
Belligerent, meddlesome thing!
Wherever he goes as a guest
He is sure to remain as a King.

—MARY ISABELLA FORSYTH.

THE English sparrow, like the poor and the house-fly, is always with us; and since he is here to stay, let us make him useful if we can devise any means of doing so. There is no bird that gives the pupils a more difficult exercise in describing colors and markings than does he; and his wife is almost equally difficult. I have known fairly skilled ornithologists to be misled by some variation in color of the hen sparrow, and it is safe to assert that the majority of people "do not know her from Adam." The male has the top of the head gray with a patch of reddish brown on either side; the middle of the throat and upper breast is black; the sides of the throat white; the lower breast and under parts grayish white; the back is brown streaked with black; the tail is brown, rather short, and not notched at the tip; the wings are brown with two white bars and a jaunty dash of reddish brown. The female has the head grayish brown, the breast, throat and under parts grayish white; the back is brown streaked with black and dirty yellow, and she is, on the whole, a "washed out" looking lady bird. The differences in color and size between the English sparrow and the chippy are quite noticeable, as the chippy is an inch shorter and far more slender in appearance, and is especially marked by the reddish brown crown.

When feeding, the English sparrows are aggressive, and their lack of table manners make them the "goops" among all birds; in the winter they settle in noisy flocks on the street to pick up the grain undigested by the horses, or in barnyards where the grain has been scattered by the cattle. They only eat weed seeds when other food fails them in the winter, for they are a civilized bird even if they do not act so, and they much prefer the cultivated grains. It is only during the nesting season that they destroy insects to any extent; over one-half the food of nestlings is insects, such as, weevils, grasshoppers, cutworms, etc.; but this good work is largely offset by the fact that these same nestlings will soon give their grown-up energies to attacking grain fields, taking the seed after sowing, later the new grain in the milk, and later still the ripened grain in the sheaf. Wheat, oats, rye, barley, corn, sorghum and rice are thus attacked. Once I saw on the upper Nile a native boat loaded with millet which was attacked by thousands of sparrows; when driven off by the sailors they would perch on the rigging, like flies, and as soon as the men turned their backs they would drop like bullets to the deck and gobble the grain before they were again driven off. English sparrows also destroy for us the buds and blossoms of fruit trees and often attack the ripening fruit.

The introduction of the English sparrow into America is one of the greatest arguments possible in favor of nature-study; for, ignorance of nature-study methods in this single instance, costs the United States millions of dollars every year. The English sparrow is the European house sparrow and people had a theory that it was an insect eater, but never took the pains to ascertain if this theory were a fact. About 1850, some people with more zeal than wisdom introduced these birds into New York, and for twenty years afterwards there were other importations of the sparrows. In twenty years more, people discovered that they had taken great pains to establish in our country one of the worst nuisances in all Europe. In addition to all the direct damage which the English sparrows do, they are so quarrelsome that they have driven away many of our native beneficial birds from our premises, and now vociferously acclaim their presence in places which were once the haunts of birds with sweet songs. After they drive off the other birds they quarrel among themselves, and there is no rest for tired ears in their vicinity. There are various noises made by these birds which we can understand if we are willing to take the pains: The harassing chirping is their song; they squall when frightened and peep plaintively when lonesome, and make a disagreeable racket when fighting.

But to "give the devil his due" we must admit that the house sparrow is as clever as it is obnoxious, and its success is doubtless partly due to its superior cleverness and keenness. It is quick to take a hint, if sufficiently pointed; firing a shotgun twice into a flock of these birds has driven them from our premises; and tearing down their nests assiduously for a month seems to convey to them the idea that they are not welcome. Another instance of their cleverness I witnessed one day; I was watching a robin, worn and nervous with her second brood, fervently hunting earthworms in the lawn to fill the gaping mouths in the nest in the Virginia creeper shading the piazza. She finally pulled up a large, pink worm and a hen sparrow flew at her viciously; the robin dropped the worm to protect herself, and the sparrow snatched it and carried it off triumphantly to the grape arbor where she had a

Young sparrow in the nest

nest of her own full of gaping mouths. She soon came back, and at a safe distance watched the robin pull out another worm, and by the same tactics again gained the squirming prize. Three times was this repeated in an hour, and then the robin, discouraged, flew up into a Norway spruce and in a monologue of sullen cluckings tried to reason out what had happened.

The English sparrow's nest is quite in keeping with the bird's other qualities; it is usually built in a hole or box or in some protected corner beneath the eaves; it is also often built in vines on buildings and occasionally in trees. It is a good example of "fuss and feathers"; coarse straw, or any other kind of material, and feathers of hens or of other birds, mixed together without fashion or form, constitute the nest. In these sprawling nests the whitish, brown or gray-flecked eggs are laid and the young reared; and so far as I can ascertain, no one has ever counted the number of broods reared in one season. The nesting begins almost as soon as the snow is off the ground and lasts until late fall.

During the winter, the sparrows gather in flocks in villages and cities, but in the spring they scatter out through the country where they can find more grain. The only place where this bird is welcome is possibly in the heart of a great city, where no other bird could pick up a livelihood. It is a true cosmopolite and is the first bird to greet the traveler in Europe or northern Africa. These sparrows will not build in boxes suspended by a wire; and they do not like a box where there is no resting place in front of the door leading to the nest.

After the pupils have made observations upon the habits of the house sparrow, they may find, in the following books and bulletins, facts which will teach further the economic importance of this bird: Birds in Their Relation to Man, by Weed and Dearborn, p. 144. The following bulletins of the U. S. Department of Agriculture: "English Sparrow in North America;" "Relation of Sparrows to Agriculture," S. D. Judd, Bulletin 15; "The Food of Nestlings," Yearbook 1900.

LESSON

Leading thought— The English sparrow was introduced into America by people who knew nothing of its habits. It has finally over-run our whole country and, to a great extent, has driven out from towns and villages our useful American song birds and it should be discouraged and not allowed to nest around our houses and grounds. As a sparrow it has interesting habits which we should observe.

Methods— Let the pupils make their observations in the street or wherever they find the birds. The greatest value of this lesson is to teach the pupils to observe the coloring and markings of a bird accurately and describe them clearly. This is the best of training for later work with the wild birds.

Observations—

1. How many kinds of birds do you find in a flock of English sparrows?

2. The ones with the black cravat are naturally the men of the family, while their sisters, wives and mothers are less ornamented. Describe in your note-book or from memory the colors of the cock sparrow as follows: Top of head; sides of the head; the back; the tail; the wings; wing bars; throat and upper breast; lower breast and under parts.

3. Describe the hen sparrow in the same manner and note the dif-

ference in markings between the two. Are the young birds, when they first fly, like the father or the mother?

4. Compare the English sparrow with the chippy and describe the differences in size and color.

5. Is the tail when the bird is not flying, square across the end or notched?

6. What is the shape of the beak? For what sort of food is this shaped beak meant?

7. What is the food of the English sparrows and where do they find it? Describe the actions of a flock feeding in the yard or street. Are the English sparrows kindly or quarrelsome in disposition?

8. Why do the English sparrows stay in the North during the coldest of winters? Do they winter out in the country or in villages?

9. Describe by observation how they try to drive away the robins or other native birds.

10. Describe the nest of this sparrow. Of what material is it made? How is it supported? How sheltered? Is it a well-built nest?

11. Describe the eggs. How many broods are raised a year? What kind of food do the parents give the nestlings?

12. If you have ever seen these sparrows do anything interesting, describe the circumstance.

13. In what ways are these birds a nuisance to us?

14. How much of English sparrow talk do you understand?

15. How can we build bird-boxes so that the English sparrows will not try to take possession of them?

Supplementary reading— "A Street Troubadour," in *Lives of the Hunted*, Thompson Seton; *First Book of Birds*, Miller, p. 81; "Blizzard" and "Three Sparrows that live in the House," from *True Bird Stories*, Miller.

Do not tire the child with questions; lead him to question you, instead. Be sure, in any case, that he is more interested in the subject than in the questions about the subject.

The Chipping Sparrow

TEACHER'S STORY

THIS midget lives in our midst, and yet, not among all bird kind, is there one which so ignores us as does the chippy. It builds its nest about our houses, it hunts for food all over our premises, it sings like a tuneful grasshopper in our ears, it brings up its young to disregard us, and every hour of the day it "tsip-tsips" us to scorn. And, although it has well earned the name of "doorstep sparrow," since it frugally gathers the crumbs about our kitchen doors, yet it rarely becomes tame or can be induced to eat from the hand, unless it is trained so to do as a nestling.

Its cinnamon-brown cap and tiny black forehead, the gray streak over the eye and the black through it, the gray cheeks and the pale gray, unspotted breast distinguish it from the other sparrows, although its brown back streaked with darker, and brown wings and blackish tail have a very sparrowish look; the two whitish wing bars are not striking; it has a bill fitted for shelling seeds, a characteristic of all the sparrows. Despite its seed-eating bill, the chippy's food is thirty-eight per-cent insects, and everyone should read what Mr. Forbush says about the good work this little bird does in our gardens and to our trees. It takes in large numbers cabbage caterpillars, the pea louse, the beet leaf-miners, leaf hoppers, grasshoppers, cut worms, and does its best to annihilate the caterpillars of the terrible gypsy and browntail moths. In fact, it works for our benefit even in its vegetable food, as this consists largely of the seeds of weeds and undesirable grasses. It will often fly up from its perch after flies or moths, like a flycatcher; and the next time we note it, it will be hopping around hunting for the crumbs we have scattered for it on the piazza floor. The song of the chippy is more interesting to it than to us; it is a continuous performance of high, shrill, rapid notes, all alike so far as I can detect; when it utters many of these in rapid succession it is singing, but when it gives them singly they are call notes or mere conversation.

One peculiarity of the nest has given this sparrow the common name of hair-bird, for the lining is almost always of long, coarse hair, usually treasure trove from the tails of horses or cattle switched off against boards, burs or other obstacles. Of the many nests I have examined, black horsehair was the usual lining; but two nests in our yard show the chippy to be a resourceful bird; evidently the hair market was exhausted and the soft, dead needles of the white pine were used instead and made a most satisfactory lining. The nest is tiny and shallow; the outside is of fine grass or rootlets carefully but not closely woven together; it is placed in vine or tree, usually not more than ten or fifteen feet from the ground; a vine of a piazza is a favorite nesting site. Once a bold pair built directly above the entrance to our front door and mingled cheerfully with other visitors. Usually, however, the nest is so hidden that it is not discovered until after the leaves have fallen. The eggs are light blue tinged with green, with fine, purplish brown specks or markings scrawled about the larger end.

The chippy comes to us in April and usually raises two broods of from three to five "piggish" youngsters, which even after they are fully grown follow pertinaciously their tired and "frazzled out" parents and beg to be fed; the chippy parents evidently have no idea of discipline but indulge their teasing progeny until our patience, at least, is exhausted. The young differ from the parents in having streaked breasts and lacking the reddish crown. In the fall the chippy parents lose their red-brown caps and have streaked ones instead; and then they fare forth in flocks for a seed-harvest in the fields. Thereafter our chippy is a stranger to us; we do not know it in its new garb, and it dodges into the bushes as we pass, as if it had not tested our harmlessness on our own door-stone.

Reference— Wild Life, Ingersoll, p. 132.

LESSON

Leading thought— The chipping sparrow is a cheerful and useful little neighbor. It builds a nest, lined with horsehair, in the shrubbery and vines about our homes and works hard in ridding our gardens of insect pests and seeds of weeds.

Methods— Begin this lesson with a nest of the chippy, which is so unmistakable that it may be identified when found in the winter. Make the study of this nest so interesting that the pupils will wait anxiously to watch for the birds which made it. As soon as the chippies appear, the questions should be asked, a few at a time, giving the children several weeks for the study.

THE NEST

OBSERVATIONS—

1. Where was this nest found? How high from the ground?

2. Was it under shelter? How was it supported?

3. Of what material is the outside of the nest? How is it fastened together? How do you suppose the bird wove this material together?

4. Of what material is the lining? Why is the bird that built this nest called the "hair bird?" From what animal do you think the lining of the nest came? How do you suppose the bird got it?

5. Do you think the nest was well hidden when the leaves were about it? Measure the nest across and also its depth; do you think the bird that made it is as large as the English sparrow?

Chipping Sparrow with nestlings

THE BIRD

6. How can you tell the chippy from the English sparrow?

7. Describe in your note-book or orally the colors of the chippy as follows: beak, forehead, crown, marks above and through the eyes, cheeks, throat, breast, wings and tail. Note if the wings have whitish bars and how many.

8. Describe the shape of the beak as compared with that of the robin. What is this shaped bill meant for?

9. What is the food of the chippy? Why has it been called the door-step-sparrow?

10. Note if the chippy catches flies or moths on the wing like the phoebe-bird.

11. Why should we protect the chippy and try to induce it to live near our gardens?

12. Does it run or hop when seeking food on the ground?

13. How early in the season does the chippy appear and where does it spend the winter?

14. Can you describe the chippy's song? How do you think it won the name of chipping sparrow?

15. If you have the luck to find a pair of chippies nesting, keep a diary of your observations in your note-book covering the following points: Do both parents build the nest? How is the frame-work laid?

Baby Chipping Sparrow, it weighs 5 grams

How is the finishing done? The number and color of the eggs? Do both parents feed the young? How do young chippies act when they first leave the nest? How large are the young birds before the parents stop feeding them? What are the differences in color and markings between parents and young?

THE FIELD-SPARROW

A bubble of music floats, the slope of the hillside over;
A little wandering sparrow's notes; and the bloom of yarrow and clover,
And the smell of sweet-fern and the bayberry leaf,
On his ripple of song are stealing,
For he is a cheerful thief, the wealth of the fields revealing.
One syllable, clear and soft as a raindrop's silvery patter,
Or a tinkling fairy-bell; heard aloft, in the midst of the merry chatter
Of robin and linnet and wren and jay, one syllable, oft repeated;
He has but a word to say, and of that he will not be cheated.
The singer I have not seen; but the song I arise and follow
The brown hills over, the pastures green, and into the sunlit hollow.
With a joy that his life unto mine has lent, I can feel my glad eyes glisten,
Though he hides in his happy tent, while I stand outside, and listen.
This way would I also sing, my dear little hillside neighbor!
A tender carol of peace to bring to the sunburnt fields of labor
Is better than making a loud ado; trill on, amid clover and yarrow!
There's a heart-beat echoing you, and blessing you, blithe little sparrow!

—LUCY LARCOM.

The Song Sparrow

TEACHER'S STORY

"He does not wear a Joseph's coat of many colors, smart and gay
His suit is Quaker brown and gray, with darker patches at his throat.
And yet of all the well-dressed throng, not one can sing so brave a song.
It makes the pride of looks appear a vain and foolish thing to hear
His 'Sweet, sweet, sweet, very merry cheer.'
A lofty place he does not love, he sits by choice and well at ease
In hedges and in little trees, that stretch their slender arms above
The meadow brook; and then he sings till all the field with pleasure rings;
And so he tells in every ear, that lowly homes to heaven are near
In 'Sweet, sweet, sweet, very merry cheer.'"

—HENRY VAN DYKE.

CHILDREN should commit to memory the poem from which the above stanzas were taken; seldom in literature have detailed accurate observation and poetry been so happily combined as in these verses. The lesson might begin in March when we are all listening eagerly for bird voices, and the children should be asked to look out for a little, brown bird which sings, "Sweet, sweet, sweet, very merry cheer," or, as Thoreau interprets it, "Maids! Maids! Maids! Hang on the teakettle, teakettle-ettle-ettle." In early childhood I learned to distinguish

121

The eggs are bluish white with many brown markings

Newly hatched song sparrow nestlings

A crowded nest

this sparrow by its "Teakettle" song. Besides this song, it has others quite as sweet; and when alarmed it utters a sharp "T'chink, t'chink."

The song sparrow prefers the neighborhood of brooks and ponds which are bordered with bushes, and also the hedges planted by nature along rail or other field fences, and it has a special liking for the shrubbery about gardens. Its movements and flight are very characteristic; it usually sits on the tip-top of a shrub or low tree when it sings, but when disturbed never rises in the air but drops into a low flight and plunges into a thicket with a defiant twitch of the tail which says plainly, "Find me if you can."

The color and markings of this bird are typical of the sparrows. The head is a warm brown with a gray streak along the center of the crown and one above each eye, with a dark line through the eye. The back is brown with darker streaks. The throat is white with a dark spot on either side; the breast is white spotted with brown with a large, dark blotch at its very center; this breast blotch distinguishes this bird from all other sparrows. The tail and wings are brown and without buff or white bars or other markings. The tail is long, rounded and very expressive of emotions, and makes the bird look more slender than the English sparrow.

The nest is usually placed on the ground or in low bushes not more than five feet from the ground; it varies much in both size and material; it is sometimes constructed of coarse weeds and grasses; and sometimes only fine grass is used. Sometimes it is lined with hair, and again, with fine grass; sometimes it is deep, but occasionally is shallow. The eggs have a whitish ground-color tinged with blue or green, but are so blotched and marked with brown that they are safe from observation of enemies. The nesting season begins in May, and there are usually three and sometimes four broods; but so far as I have observed, a nest is never used for two consecutive broods. The song sparrow stays with us in New York State very late in the fall, and a few stay in sheltered places all winter. The quality in this bird which endears him to us all is the spirit of song which stays with him; his sweet trill may be heard almost any month of the year, and he has a charming habit of singing in his dreams, if sudden noise disturbs his slumber.

The song sparrow is not only the dearest of little neighbors, but it also works lustily for our good and for its own food at the same time. It destroys cutworms, plant-lice, caterpillars, canker-worms, ground beetles, grasshoppers and flies; in winter it destroys thousands of weed seeds, which otherwise would surely plant themselves to our undoing. Every boy and girl should take great pains to drive away stray cats and to teach the family puss not to meddle with birds; for cats are the worst of all the song sparrow's enemies, destroying thousands of its nestlings every year.

Lesson

Leading thought— The beautiful song of this sparrow is heard earlier in the spring than the notes of bluebird or robin. The dark blotch in the center of its speckled breast distinguishes this sparrow from all others; it is very beneficial and should be protected from cats.

Methods— All the observations of the song sparrow must be made in the field, and they are easily made because the bird builds near

Sparrow singing

houses, in gardens, and in the shrubbery. Poetry and other literature about the song sparrow should be given to the pupils to read or to memorize.

Observations—

1. Have you noticed a little brown bird singing a very sweet song in the early spring? Did the song sound as if set to the words "Little Maid! Little Maid! Little Maid! Put on the teakettle, tea-kettle-ettle-ettle?"

2. Where was this bird when you heard him singing? How high was he perched above the ground? What other notes did you hear him utter?

3. Describe the colors and markings of the song sparrow on head, back, throat, breast, wings and tail. Is this bird as large as the English sparrow? What makes it look more slim?

4. How can you distinguish the song sparrow from the other sparrows? When disturbed does it fly up or down? How does it gesture with its tail as it disappears in the bushes?

5. Where and of what material does the song sparrow build its nest?

6. What colors and markings are on the eggs? Do you think these colors and markings are useful in concealing the eggs when the mother bird leaves the nest?

7. How late in the season do you see the song sparrows and hear their songs?

8. How can we protect these charming little birds and induce them to build near our houses?

9. What is the food of the song sparrows and how do they benefit our fields and gardens?

Supplementary reading— Our Birds and Their Nestlings, Walker, pp. 43, 49, 50, 52; *Second Book of Birds*, Miller, p. 80; *Birds of Song and Story*, Grinnell, p. 73; *The Song Sparrow*, Van Dyke; *Birds Through an Opera Glass*, Merriam, p. 66; *Field Book of Wild Birds*, Mathews, p. 109; *Wild Life*, Ingersoll, p. 144; Audubon Leaflet No. 31.

THE SING-AWAY BIRD

Have you ever heard of the Sing-away bird,
That sings where the Runaway River
Runs down with its rills from the bald-headed hills
That stand in the sunshine and shiver?
"Oh, sing! sing-away! sing-away!"
How the pines and the birches are stirred
By the trill of the Sing-away bird!
And the bald-headed hills, with their rocks and their rills,
To the tune of his rapture are ringing;
And their faces grow young, all the gray mists among,
While the forests break forth into singing.
"Oh sing! sing-away! sing-away!"
And the river runs singing along;
And the flying winds catch up the song.
'Twas a white-throated sparrow, that sped a light arrow
Of song from his musical quiver,
And it pierced with its spell every valley and dell
On the banks of the Runaway River.
"Oh, sing! sing-away! sing-away!"
The song of the wild singer had
The sound of a soul that is glad.

—LUCY LARCOM.

Northern Mockingbird

The Mockingbird

TEACHER'S STORY

AMONG all the vocalists in the bird world, the mockingbird is un-rivaled in the variety and richness of his repertoire; and he has thus won his place among men, convincing many ignorant people by the means of his voice that a bird is good for something besides "vict-uals." The mockingbirds go as far north as southern New England, but they are found at their best in the Southern States and in California. On the Gulf Coast the mockers begin singing in February; in warmer climates they sing almost the year through. During the nesting sea-son, the father mocker is so busy with his cares and duties during the day, that he does not have time to sing and so devotes the nights to serenading; he may sing almost all night long if there is moonlight, but even on dark nights he gives now and then a happy, sleepy song. Not all mockingbirds are mockers; some sing their own song which is rich and beautiful; while others learn, in addition, not only the songs of other birds, but their call notes as well. One authority noted a mocker which imitated the songs of twenty species of birds during a ten-minute performance. When singing, the mocker shows his relationship to the brown thrasher by lifting the head and depressing and jerking the tail. A good mocker will learn a tune, or parts of it, if it is whistled often enough in his hearing; he will also imitate other sounds and will often improve on a song he has learned from another bird by introducing frills of his own; when learning a song, he sits silent and listens intently, but will not try to sing it until it is learned.

Mockingbird eggs in a nest.

Although the mockingbirds live in wild places, they prefer the haunts of men, taking up their home sites in gardens and cultivated grounds. Their flight is rarely higher than the tree tops and is decidedly jerky in character with much twitching of the long tail. For nesting sites, they choose thickets or the lower branches of trees, being especially fond of orange trees; the nest is usually from four to twenty feet from the ground. The foundation of the nest is made of sticks, grasses and weed stalks interlaced and crisscrossed; on these is built the nest of softer materials, such as rootlets, horsehair, cotton, or in fact, anything suitable which is at hand. The nest is often in plain sight, since the mocker trusts to his strength as a fighter to protect it. He will attack cats with great ferocity and vanquish them; he will kill snakes; often good-sized black snakes have been known to end thus. The mocker, in making his attack, hovers above his enemy and strikes it at the back of the head or neck; he will also drive away birds much larger than himself.

The female lays from four to six pale greenish or bluish eggs blotched with brown and which hatch in about two weeks; then comes a period of hard work for the parents, as both are indefatigable in catching insects to feed the young. The mocker, by the way, is a funny sight when he is chasing a beetle on the ground, lifting his wings in a pugnacious fashion. The mockers often raise three broods a season; the young birds have spotted breasts, showing their relationship to the thrasher.

As a wooer, the mocker is a bird of much ceremony and dances into his lady's graces. Mrs. F. W. Rowe, in describing this, says that the birds stand facing each other with heads and tails erect and wings drooping; "then the dance would begin, and this consisted of the two hopping sideways in the same direction and in rather a straight line a few inches at a time, always keeping directly opposite each other and about the same distance apart. They would *chassez* this way four or five feet, then go back over the same line in the same manner." Mrs. Rowe also observed that the male mockers have hunting preserves of their own, not allowing any other males of their species in these precincts. The boundary was sustained by tactics of both offense and defense; but certain other species of birds were allowed to trespass without reproof.

Maurice Thompson describes in a delightful manner the "mounting" and "dropping" songs of the mocker which occur during the wooing season. The singer flits up from branch to branch of a tree, singing as he goes, and finally on the topmost bough gives his song of triumph to the world; then, reversing the process, he falls backward from spray to spray, as if drunk with the ecstasy of his own song, which is an exquisitely soft "gurgling series of notes, liquid and sweet, that seem to express utter rapture."

The mockingbirds have the same colors in both sexes; the head is black, the back is ashy-gray; the tail and wings are so dark brown that they look black; the tail is very long and has the outer tail feathers entirely white and the two next inner ones are white for more than half their length; the wings have a strikingly broad, white bar, which is very noticeable when the bird is flying. The under parts and breast are grayish white; the beak and legs are blackish. The food of the mockingbirds is about half insects and half fruit. They live largely on the berries of the red cedar, myrtle and holly, and we must confess are often too devoted to the fruits in our orchards and gardens; but let us put down to their credit that they do their best to exterminate the cot-

The brown thrasher, a close relative of the mockingbird, is also an accomplished musician

ton boll caterpillars and moths, and also many other insects injurious to crops.

The mocker is full of tricks and is distinctly a bird of humor. He will frighten other birds by screaming like a hawk and then seem to chuckle over the joke.

Sidney Lanier describes him well:

Whate'er birds did or dreamed, this bird could say.
Then down he shot, bounced airily along
The sward, twitched in a grasshopper, made song
Midflight, perched, prinked, and to his art again.

LESSON

Leading thought— The mockingbird is the only one of our common birds that sings regularly at night. It imitates the songs of other birds and has also a beautiful song of its own. When feeding their nestlings, the mockers do us great service by destroying insect pests.

Method— Studies of this bird are best made individually by the pupils through watching the mockers which haunt the houses and shrubbery. If there are mockingbirds near the schoolhouse the work can be done in the most ideal way by keeping records in the school of all the observations made by the pupils, thus bringing out an interesting mockingbird story. The experiment in teaching songs to the birds may best be made with pet mockers.

Observations—

1. At what months of the year and for how many months does the mockingbird sing in this locality?

2. Does he sing only on moonlight nights? Does he sing all night?

3. Can you distinguish the true mockingbird song from the songs which he has learned from other birds? Describe the actions of a mocker when he is singing.

4. How many songs of other birds have you heard a mocker give and what are the names of these birds?

5. Have you ever taught a mocker a tune by whistling it in his presence? If so, tell how long before he learned it and how he acted while learning.

6. Describe the flight of the mockingbirds. Do they fly high in the air like crows?

7. Do these birds like best to live in wild places or about houses and gardens?

8. Where do they choose sites for their nests? Do they make an effort to hide the nest? If not, why?

9. Of what material is the nest made? How is it lined? How far from the ground is it placed?

10. What are the colors of the eggs? How many are usually laid? How long before they hatch?

11. Give instances of the parents' devotion to the young birds.

12. Have you seen two mockingbirds dancing before each other just before the nesting season?

13. In the spring have you heard a mocker sing while mounting from the lower to the upper branches of a tree and then, after pouring forth his best song, fall backward with a sweet, gurgling song as if intoxicated with his music?

14. How many broods does a pair of mockers raise during one season? How does the color of the breast of the young differ from that of the parent?

15. How does the father bird protect the nestlings from other birds, cats and snakes?

16. Does the mocker select certain places for his own hunting grounds and drive off other mockers which trespass?

17. Describe the colors of the mockingbird as follows: Beak, head, back, tail, wings, throat, breast, under parts and feet.

18. What is the natural food of the mockingbirds and how do they benefit the farmer? How does the mocker act when attacking a ground beetle?

19. Have you seen mockingbirds frighten other birds by imitating the cry of a hawk? Have you seen them play other kinds of tricks?

20. Write a little story which shall include your own observations on the ways of pet mockingbirds which you have known.

Supplementary reading— True Bird Stories, Miller, p. 142; Bob, by Sidney Lanier; Second Book of Birds, Miller, p. 34; Birds of Song and Story, Grinnell, p. 29; Stories About Birds, Kirby, p. 94.

"*Soft and low the song began: I scarcely caught it as it ran*
Through the melancholy trill of the plaintive whip-poor-will,
Through the ringdove's gentle wail, chattering jay and whistling quail,
Sparrow's twitter, catbird's cry, redbird's whistle, robin's sigh;
Blackbird, bluebird, swallow, lark, each his native note might mark.
Oft he tried the lesson o'er, each time louder than before;
Burst at length the finished song, loud and clear it poured along;
All the choir in silence heard, hushed before this wondrous bird.
All transported and amazed, scarcely breathing, long I gazed.
Now it reached the loudest swell; lower, lower, now it fell,—
Lower, lower, lower still, scarce it sounded o'er the rill."

—JOSEPH RODMAN DRAKE.

The Catbird

TEACHER'S STORY

"The Catbird sings a crooked song, in minors that are flat,
And, when he can't control his voice he mews just like a cat,
Then nods his head and whisks his tail and lets it go at that."

—OLIVER DAVIE.

AS a performer, the catbird distinctly belongs to the vaudeville, even going so far as to appear in slate-colored tights. His specialties range from the most exquisite song to the most strident of scolding notes; his nasal "n-y-a-a-h, n-y-a-a-h" is not so very much like the cat's mew after all, but when addressed to the intruder it means "get out;" and not in the whole gamut of bird notes is there another which so quickly inspires the listener with this desire. I once trespassed upon the territory of a well-grown catbird family and the squalling that ensued was ear-splitting; as I retreated, the triumphant youngsters followed me for a few rods with every sign of triumph in their actions and voices; they obviously enjoyed my apparent fright. The catbirds have rather a pleasant "cluck, cluck" when talking to each other, hidden in the bushes, and they also have a variety of other notes. The true song of the catbird, usually given in the early morning, is very beautiful. Mr. Mathews thinks it is a medley gathered from other birds, but it seems to me very individual. However, true to his vaudeville training, this bird is likely to introduce into the middle or at the end of his exquisite song some phrase that suggests his cat call. He is, without doubt, a true mocker and will often imitate the robin's song, and also if opportunity offers learns to converse fluently in chicken language. One spring morning, I heard outside my window the mellow song of the cardinal, which is a rare visitor in New York, but there was no mistaking the "tor-re-do, tor-re-do." I sprang from my bed and rushed to the window only to see a catbird singing the cardinal song, and thus telling me that he had come from the sunny South and the happy companionship of these brilliant birds. Often when the catbird is singing, he sits on the topmost spray of some shrub lifting his head and depressing his tail, like a brown thrasher; and again, he sings completely hidden in the thicket.

In appearance the catbird is tailor-made, belonging to the same social class as the cedar-bird and the barn swallow. However, it affects quiet colors, and its well-fitting costume is all slate-gray except the top of the head and the tail which are black; the feathers beneath the base of the tail are brownish. The catbird is not so large as the robin, and is of very different shape; it is far more slender and has a long, emotional tail. The way the catbird twitches and tilts its tail, as it hops along the ground or alights in a bush, is very characteristic. It is a particularly alert and nervous bird, always on the watch for intruders, and the first to give warning to all other birds of their approach. It is a good fighter in defending its nest, and there are several observed instances where it has fought to defend the nest of other species of birds; and it has gone even further in its philanthropy, by feeding their orphaned nestlings.

The catbird chooses a nesting site in a low tree or shrub or brier, where the nest is built usually about four feet from the ground. The nest looks untidy, but is strongly made of sticks, coarse grass, weeds, bark strips and occasionally paper; it is lined with soft roots and is almost always well hidden in dense foliage. The eggs are from three

*The catbird lays three to five eggs of a rich greenish blue in a well
constructed nest in a dense thicket*

to five in number and are dark greenish blue. Both parents work hard
feeding the young and for this purpose destroy many insects which
we can well spare. Sixty-two per cent of the food of the young has been
found in one instance to be cutworms, showing what a splendid work
the parents do in our gardens. In fact, during a large part of the summer, while these birds are rearing their two broods, they benefit us
greatly by destroying the insect pests; and although later they may
attack our fruits and berries, it almost seems as if they had earned
the right to their share. If we only had the wisdom to plant along the
fences some elderberries or Russian mulberries, the catbirds as well
as the robins would feed upon them instead of the cultivated fruits.

The catbirds afford a striking example for impressing upon children that each species of birds haunts certain kinds of places. The catbirds are never found in deep woods nor in open fields, but always near
low thickets along streams, and in shrubbery along fences, in tangles
of vines, and especially do they like to build about our gardens, if we
protect them. They are very fond of bathing, and if fresh water is given
them for this purpose, we may have opportunity to witness the most
thorough bath a bird can take. A catbird takes a long time to bathe and
preen its feathers and indulges in most luxurious sun baths and thus
deservedly earns the epithet of "well-groomed;" it is one of the most

A catbird on her nest

intelligent of all our birds and soon learns "what is what," and repays in the most surprising way the trouble of careful observation.

LESSON

Leading thought— The catbird has a beautiful song as well as the harsh "miou," and can imitate other birds, although not so well as the mockingbird. It builds in low thickets and shrubbery and during the nesting season is of great benefit to our gardens.

Methods— First, let the pupils study and report upon the songs, scoldings and other notes of this our northern mockingbird; then let them describe its appearance and habits. Of course, the study must be made outside of school hours in the field.

Observations—

1. Do you think the squall of the catbird sounds like the mew of a cat? When does the bird use this note and what for? What other notes have you heard it utter?

2. Describe as well as you can the catbird's true song. Are there any

135

harsh notes in it? Where does he sit while singing? Describe his actions while singing.

3. Have you ever heard the catbird imitate the songs of other birds or other noises?

4. Describe the catbird as follows: its size and shape compared to the robin; the color and shape of head, beak, wings, tail, breast and under parts.

5. Describe its peculiar actions and its characteristic movements.

6. Where do catbirds build their nests? How high from the ground? What material is used? Is the nest compact and carefully finished? Is it hidden?

7. What is the color of the eggs? Do both parents care for the young?

8. What is the food of the catbird? Why is it an advantage to us to have catbirds build in our gardens?

9. Do you ever find catbirds in the deep woods or out in the open meadows? Where do you find them?

10. Put out a pan of water where the catbirds can use it and then watch them make their toilets and describe the process. Describe how they take sun baths.

Supplementary reading—"Monsieur Mischief," *Nestlings of Forest and Marsh, Wheelock; Our Birds and Their Nestlings,* Walker, pp. 167, 174; *Second Book of Birds,* Miller, p. 37; *Songs of Nature,* Burroughs, p. 172; *Birds of Song and Story,* Grinnell, p. 36.

> "He sits on a branch of yon blossoming bush,
> This madcap cousin of robin and thrush,
> And sings without ceasing the whole morning long;
> Now wild, now tender, the wayward song
> That flows from his soft, gray, fluttering throat;
> But often he stops in his sweetest note,
> And, shaking a flower from the blossoming bough,
> Drawls out, "Mi-eu, mi-ow!""
>   —"THE CATBIRD," EDITH M. THOMAS

ANDY MORFFEW (CC BY 2.0)

The Belted Kingfisher

TEACHER'S STORY

THIS patrol of our streams and lake shores, in his cadet uniform, is indeed a military figure as well as a militant personality. As he sits upon his chosen branch overhanging some stream or lake shore, his crest abristle, his keen eye fixed on the water below, his whole bearing alert, one must acknowledge that this fellow puts "ginger" into his environment, and that the spirit which animates him is very far from the *"dolce far niente"* which permeates the ordinary fisherman. However, he does not fish for fun but for business; his keen eye catches the gleam of a moving fin and he darts from his perch, holds himself for a moment on steady wings above the surface of the water, to be sure of his quarry, and then there is a dash and a splash and he returns to his perch with the wriggling fish in his strong beak; he at once proceeds to beat its life out against a branch and then to swallow it sensibly, head first, so that the fins will not prick his throat nor the scales rasp it. He swallows the entire fish, trusting to his internal organs to select

A large sharply pointed bill and a good aim behind it is all the equipment this feathered fisherman needs to catch his food

the nourishing part; and later he gulps up a ball of the indigestible scales and bones.

The kingfisher is very different in form from an ordinary bird; he is larger than a robin, and his head and fore parts are much larger in proportion; this is the more noticeable because of the long feathers of the head which he lifts into a crest, and because of the shortness of the tail. The beak is very long and strong in order to seize the fish and hold it fast; but the legs are short and weak; the third and fourth toes are grown together for a part of their length; perhaps this is of use to the bird in pushing earth from the burrow, when excavating. The kingfisher has no need for running and hopping, like the robin and, therefore, does not need the robin's strong legs and feet. His colors are beautiful and harmonious; the upper parts are grayish blue, the throat and collar white, as is also the breast, which has a bluish gray band across the upper part, this giving the name of the Belted Kingfisher to the bird. The feathers of the wings are tipped with white and the tail feathers narrowly barred with white. The under side of the body is white in the males, while in the females it is somewhat chestnut in color. There is a striking white spot just in front of the eye.

The kingfisher parents build their nest in a burrow which they tunnel horizontally in a bank; sometimes there is a vestibule of several feet before the nest is reached, and at other times it is built very close to the opening. Both parents are industrious in catching fish for their nestlings, but the burden of this duty falls heaviest upon the male. Many fish bones are found in the nest, and they seem so

Kingfisher's foot. This shows the weak toes; the third and fourth are joined together, which undoubtedly assists the bird in pushing out soil when excavating.

clean and white that they have been regarded as nest lining. Wonderful tales are told of the way the English kingfishers use fish bones to support the earth above their nests, and tributes have been paid to their architectural skill. But it is generally conceded that the lining of fish bones in nests of our kingfisher is incidental, since the food of the young is largely fish, although frogs, insects and other creatures are often eaten with relish. It is interesting to note the process by which the young kingfisher gets its skill in fishing. I have often seen one dive horizontally for a yard or two beneath the water and come up indignant and sputtering because the fish had escaped. It was fully two weeks after this before this one learned to drop like a bullet on its quarry.

The note of the kingfisher is a loud rattle, not especially pleasant close at hand, but not unmusical at a little distance. It is a curious coincidence that it sounds very much like the clicking of the fisherman's reel; it is a sound that conjures visions of shade-dappled streams and the dancing, blue waters of tree-fringed lakes and ponds.

There seems to be a division of fishing ground among the kingfishers, one bird never trespassing upon its neighbor's preserves. Unless it be the parent pair working near each other for the nestlings, or the nestlings still under their care, we never see two kingfishers in the same immediate locality.

References— *The Bird*, p. 97; *The Bird Book*, pp. 154, 444.

LESSON

Leading thought— The kingfisher is fitted by form of body and beak to be a fisherman.

Methods— If the school be near a stream or pond the following observations may be made by the pupils; otherwise let the boys who go fishing make a study of the bird and report to the school.

Observations—

1. Where have you seen the kingfisher? Have you often seen it on a certain branch which is its favorite perch? Is this perch near the water? What is the advantage of this position to the bird?

2. What does the kingfisher feed upon? How does it obtain its food? Describe the actions of one of these birds while fishing.

3. With what weapons does the kingfisher secure the fish? How long is its beak compared with the rest of its body? How does it kill the fish? Does it swallow the fish head or tail first? Why? Does it tear off the scales or fins before swallowing it? How does it get rid of these and the bones of the fish?

4. Which is the larger, the kingfisher or the robin? Describe the difference in shape of the bodies of these two birds; also in the size and shape of feet and beaks and explain why they are so different in form. What is there peculiar about the kingfisher's feet? Do you know which two toes are grown together?

5. What are the colors of the kingfisher in general? The colors of head, sides of head, collar, back, tail, wings, throat, breast and under parts? Is there a white spot near the eye? If so, where? Do you know the difference in colors between the parent birds?

6. Where is the nest built? How is it lined?

7. What is the note of the kingfisher? Does it give it while perching or while on the wing? Do you ever find more than one kingfisher on the same fishing grounds?

Supplementary reading— *The Second Book of Birds*, Chapter XXX; "The Halycon Birds," *Child's Study of the Classics*; Audubon Leaflet No. 19; "Kooskosemus," Long; *American Birds*, Finley.

A kingfisher eats a tadpole

THE KINGFISHER (OF ENGLAND)

For the handsome Kingfisher, go not to the tree,
No bird of the field or the forest is he;
In the dry river rock he did never abide,
And not on the brown heath all barren and wide.
He lives where the fresh, sparkling waters are flowing,
Where the tall heavy Typha and Loosestrife are growing;
By the bright little streams that all joyfully run
Awhile in the shadow, and then in the sun.
He lives in a hole that is quite to his mind,
With the green mossy Hazel roots firmly entwined;
Where the dark Alder-bough waves gracefully o'er,
And the Sword-flag and Arrow-head grow at his door.
There busily, busily, all the day long,
He seeks for small fishes the shallows among;
For he builds his nest of the pearly fish-bone,
Deep, deep, in the bank, far retired, and alone.
Then the brown Water-Rat from his burrow looks out,
To see what his neighbor Kingfisher's about;
And the green Dragon-fly, flitting slowly away,
Just pauses one moment to bid him good-day.
O happy Kingfisher! What care should he know,
By the clear, pleasant streams, as he skims to and fro,
Now lost in the shadow, now bright in the sheen
Of the hot summer sun, glancing scarlet and green!
                                        —Mary Howitt.

A whiskered screech owl

The Screech Owl

TEACHER'S STORY

"Disquiet yourselves not. 'Tis nothing but a little, downy owl."
—SHELLEY.

OF all the fascinating sounds to be heard at night in the woods, the screech owl's song is surely the most so; its fascination does not depend on music but upon the chills which it sends up and down the spine of the listener, thus attacking a quite different set of nerves than do other bird songs. The weird wail, tremulous and long drawn out, although so blood-curdling, is from the standpoint of the owlet the most beautiful music in the world; by means of it he calls to his mate, cheering her with the assurance of his presence in the world; evidently she is not a nervous creature. The screech owls are likely to sing at night during any part of the year; nor should we infer that when they are singing they are not hunting, for perchance their music frightens their victims into fatal activity. Although the note is so unmistakable, yet there is great variation in the songs of individuals, the great variety of quavers in the song offering ample opportunity for the expres-

Eastern screech owl

sion of individuality. Moreover, these owls often give themselves over to tremulous whispering and they emphasize excitement by snapping their beaks in an alarming manner.

Any bird that is flying about and singing in the night time must be able to see where it is going, and the owls have special adaptations for this. The eyes are very large and the yellow iris opens and closes about the pupil quite similar to the arrangement in the cat's eye, except that the pupil in the owl's eye is round when contracted instead of elongated; in the night this pupil is expanded until it covers most of the eye. The owl does not need to see behind and at the sides, since it does not belong to the birds which are the victims of other birds and animals of prey. The owl is a bird that hunts instead of being hunted, and it needs only to focus its eyes on the creature it is chasing. Thus, its eyes are in the front of the head like our own; but it can see behind, in case of need, for the head turns upon the neck as if it were fitted on a ball-bearing joint. I have often amused myself by walking around a captive screech owl, which would follow me with its eyes by turning the head until it almost made the circle, then the head would twist back with such lightning rapidity that I could hardly detect the movement; it seemed almost as if the head was on a pivot and could be moved around and around indefinitely. Although the owl, like the cat, has eyes fitted for night hunting, it can also see fairly well during the daytime.

A beak with the upper mandible ending in a sharp hook signifies that its owner lives upon other animals and needs to rend and tear flesh. The owl's beak thus formed is somewhat buried in the feathers of the face, which gives it a striking resemblance to a Roman nose. This, with the great, staring, round eyes, bestows upon the owl an appearance of great wisdom. But it is not the beak which the owl uses for a weapon of attack; its strong feet and sharp, curved claws are its weapons for striking the enemy and also for grappling with its prey. The outer toe can be moved back at will, so that in grasping its prey or its perch, two toes may be directed forward and two backward, thus giving a stronger hold.

The ear is very different in form from the ear of other birds; instead of being a mere hole opening into the internal ear, it consists of a fold of skin forming a channel which extends from above the eye around to the side of the throat. (See The Bird, Beebe, p. 217). Thus equipped, while hunting in the dark the owl is able to hear any least rustle of mouse or bird and to know in which direction to descend upon it. There has been no relation established between the ear tufts of the screech owl and its ears, so far as I know, but the way the bird lifts the tufts when it is alert, always suggests that this movement in some way opens up the ear.

In color there are two types among the screech owls, one reddish brown, the other gray. The back is streaked with black, the breast is marked with many shaft-lines of black. The whole effect of the owl's plumage makes it resemble a branch of a tree or a part of the bark, and thus it is protected from prying eyes, during the daytime when it is sleeping. Its plumage is very fluffy and its wing feathers, instead of being stiff to the very edge, have soft fringes which cushion the stroke upon the air. The owl's flight is, therefore, absolutely noiseless and the bird is thus able to swoop down upon its prey without giving warning of its approach.

The screech owls are partial to old apple orchards for nesting sites. They will often use an abandoned nest of a woodpecker; the eggs are

A barn or monkey-faced owl

almost as round as marbles and as white as chalk, showing very clearly that they are laid within a dark hole, otherwise their color would attract the eyes of enemies. There are usually four eggs; the fubsy little owlets climb out of their home cave by the end of May and are the funniest little creatures imaginable. They make interesting but decidedly snappy pets; they can be fed on insects and raw beef. It is most interesting to see one wake up late in the afternoon after its daytime sleep. All day it has sat motionless upon its perch with its toes completely covered with its fluffy feather skirt. Suddenly its eyes open, the round pupils enlarging or contracting with great rapidity as if adjusting themselves to the amount of light. When the owl winks it is like a moon in eclipse, so large are the eyes, and so entirely are they obscured by the lids which seem like circular curtains. When it yawns, its wide bill absurdly resembles a human mouth, and the yawn is very human in its expression. It then stretches its wings and it is astonishing how long this wing can be extended below the feet. It then begins its toilet. It dresses its feathers with its short beak, nibbling industriously in the fluff; it scratches its under parts and breast with its bill, then cleans the bill with its foot, meanwhile moving the head up and down as if in an attempt to see better its surroundings.

The owls are loyal lovers and are said to remain mated through life, the twain being very devoted to their nests and nestlings. Sometimes the two wise-looking little parents sit together on the eggs, a most happy way to pass the wearisome incubation period.

The screech owls winter in the north and they are distinctly foresighted in preparing for winter. They have often been observed catching mice, during the late fall, and placing them in some hollow tree for cold storage, whence they may be taken in time of need. Their food consists to some extent of insects, especially night-flying moths and beetles, also caterpillars and grasshoppers. However, the larger part of their food is mice; sometimes small birds are caught and the English sparrow is a frequent victim. Chickens are rarely taken, except when small, since this owlet is not as long as a robin. It swallows its quarry as whole as possible, trusting to its inner organs to do the sifting and selecting. Later it throws up pellets of the indigestible bones, hair, etc. By the study of these pellets, found under owl roosts, the scientists have been able to determine the natural food of the bird, and they all unite in assuring us that the screech owl does the farmer much more good than harm, since it feeds so largely upon creatures which destroy his crops.

LESSON

Leading thought— This owl is especially adapted to get its prey at night. It feeds largely on field mice, grasshoppers, caterpillars and other injurious insects and is therefore the friend of the farmer.

Method— This lesson should begin when the children first hear the cry of this owl; and an owlet in captivity is a fascinating object for the children to observe. However, it is so important that the children learn the habits of this owl that the teacher is advised to hinge the lesson on any observation whatever made by the pupils, and illustrate it with pictures and stories.

Observations—

1. Have you ever heard the screech owl? At what time of the day or night? Why was this? Why does the owl screech? How did you feel when listening to the owl's song?

2. Describe the owl's eyes. Are they adapted to see by night? What changes take place in them to enable the owl to see by daytime also? In what way are the owl's eyes similar to the cat's? Why is it necessary

Great Horned Owl

for an owl to see at night? Are the owl's eyes placed so that they can see at the sides like other birds? How does it see an object at the sides or behind it?

3. Note the owl's beak. For what purpose is a hooked beak? How does the owl use its beak? Why do we think that the owl looks wise?

4. Describe the feet and claws of the screech owl. What are such sharp hooked claws meant for? Does an owl on a perch always have three toes directed forward and one backward?

5. Describe the colors of the screech owl. Are all these owls of the same color? How do these colors protect the bird from its enemies?

6. How is the owl's plumage adapted to silent flight? Why is silent flight advantageous to this bird?

7. How does the owl's ear differ from the ears of other birds? Of what special advantage is this? As the owl hunts during the night, what does it do in the daytime? How and by what means does it hide itself?

8. Where does the screech owl make its nest? Do you know any-thing about the devotion of the parent owls to each other and to their

young? How many eggs are laid? What is their color? At what time of year do the little owls appear?

9. Where does the screech owl spend the winter? What do the screech owls feed upon? Do they chew their food? How do they get rid of the indigestible portion of their food? How does this habit help the scientists to know the food of the owls?

10. How does the screech owl work injury to the farmers? How does it benefit them? Does not the benefit outweigh the injury?

11. How many other kinds of owls do you know? What do you know of their habits?

Supplementary reading—Audubon Educational Leaflets, Nos. 22, 12, 14; *Second Book of Birds*, Miller, Chap. 32-3; *Familiar Wild Animals*, Lottridge; "The Boy and Hushwing," *Kindred of the Wild*; "Koos, Koos, Koos" in *Wilderness Ways*; *Wings and Fins*, chap. 19; *Heart of Oak Books*, Vol. 4, p. 51; *The Aziola*, Shelley; *American Birds*, Finley.

TWO WISE OWLS
We are two dusky owls, and we live in a tree;
Look at her,—look at me!
Look at her,—she's my mate, and the mother of three
Pretty owlets, and we
Have a warm cosy nest, just as snug as can be.

We are both very wise; for our heads, as you see,
(Look at her—look at me!)
Are as large as the heads of four birds ought to be;
And our horns, you'll agree,
Make us look wiser still, sitting here on the tree.

And we care not how gloomy the night-time may be;
We can see,—we can see
Through the forest to roam, it suits her, it suits me;
And we're free,—we are free
To bring back what we find, to our nest in the tree.

—ANONYMOUS.

The fish hawk or osprey. This hawk builds its large nest from twenty to fifty feet above the ground. It subsists almost entirely on fish

The Hawks

TEACHER'S STORY

"Above the tumult of the cañon lifted, the gray hawk breathless hung,
Or on the hill a winged shadow drifted where furze and thornbush clung."

—BRET HARTE.

IT is the teacher's duty and privilege to try to revolutionize some popular misconceptions about birds, and two birds, in great need in this respect, are the so-called hen hawks. They are most unjustly treated, largely because most farmers consider that a "hawk is a hawk," and should always be shot to save the poultry, although there is as much difference in the habits of hawks as there is in those of men. The so-called hen hawks are the red-shouldered and the red-tailed species, the latter being somewhat the larger and rarer of the two; both are very large birds; the red-shouldered has cinnamon brown epaulets, the tail blackish, crossed by five or six narrow white bars, and the wing feathers are also barred. The red-tailed species has dark brown wings, the feathers not barred, and is distinguished by its tail which is brilliant cinnamon color with a black bar across it near the end; it is silvery white beneath. When the hawk is soaring, its tail shows reddish as it wheels in the air. Both birds are brown above and whitish below, streaked with brown.

The flight of these hawks is alike and is very beautiful; it consists of soaring on outstretched wings in wide circles high in the air, and is the ideal of graceful aerial motion. In rising, the bird faces the wind and drops a little in the circle as its back turns to the leeward, and thus it climbs an invisible winding stair until it is a mere speck in the sky. This wonderful flight, on motionless wings, is what has driven to despair our inventors of airships who have not been able to fathom the mystery of it from a practical standpoint.

Red-tailed hawk

When the bird wishes to drop, it lifts and holds its wings above its back, and comes down like a lump of lead, only to catch itself whenever it chooses to begin again to climb the invisible spiral. And all this is done without fatigue, for these birds have been observed to soar thus for hours together without coming to earth. When thus soaring the two species may be distinguished from each other by their cries; the red-tailed gives a high sputtering scream, which Chapman likens to the sound of escaping steam; while the red-shouldered calls in a high not unmusical note "kee-you, kee-you" or "tee-ur, tee-ur."

The popular fallacy for the teacher to correct about these birds, is that they are enemies of the farmers. Not until one has actually been seen to catch the chickens should it be shot, for very few of them are guilty of this sin. Sixty-six per cent of the food of the red-tailed species consists of injurious animals, i. e., mice and gophers, etc., and only 7 per cent consists of poultry; the victims are probably old or disabled fowls, and fall an easy prey; this bird much prefers mice and reptiles to poultry. The more common red-shouldered hawk feeds generally on mice, snakes, frogs, fish and is very fond of grasshoppers. Ninety

The marsh harrier (formerly marsh hawk). This is a bird of the open fields. It flies low in search of rodents, reptiles, frogs, and insects. It may be identified by a white spot on the rump

per cent of its food consists of creatures which injure our crops or pastures and scarcely 1 ½ per cent is made up of poultry and game. These facts have been ascertained by the experts in the department of Agriculture at Washington who have examined the stomachs of hundreds of these hawks taken from different localities. Furthermore, Dr. Fisher states that a pair of the red-shouldered hawks bred for successive years within a few hundred yards of a poultry farm, containing 800 young chickens and 400 ducks, and the owner never saw them attempt to catch a fowl.

However, there *are* certain species of hawks which are to be feared; these are the Cooper's hawk and the sharp-shinned hawk, the first being very destructive to poultry and the latter killing many wild birds. These are both somewhat smaller than the species we are studying. They are dark gray above and have very long tails, and when flying, they flap their wings for a time and then glide a distance. They do not soar on motionless outspread pinions by the hour.

Swamp harrier eggs in nest

When hawks are seen soaring, they are likely to be hunting for mice in the meadows below them; their eyes are remarkably keen; they can see a moving creature from a great height, and can suddenly drop upon it like a thunder bolt out of a clear sky. Their wonderful eyes are far-sighted when they are circling in the sky, but as they drop, the focus of the eyes changes automatically with great rapidity, so that by the time they reach the earth they are near-sighted, a feat quite impossible for our eyes unless aided by glasses or telescope.

These so-called hen hawks will often sit motionless, for hours at a time, on some dead branch or dead tree; they are probably watching for something eatable to stir within the range of their keen vision. When seizing its prey, a hawk uses its strong feet and sharp, curved talons. All hawks keep their claws sharp and polished, even as the warrior keeps his sword bright, so as to be ready for use; the legs are covered by a growth of feathers extending down from above, looking like feather trousers. The beak is hooked and very sharp and is used for tearing apart the flesh of the quarry. When a hawk fights some larger animal or man, it throws itself over upon its back and strikes its assailant with its strong claws as well as with its beak; but the talons are its chief weapons.

Both species build a large, shallow nest of coarse sticks and grass, lined with moss, feathers, etc.; it is a rude, rough structure, and is placed in tall trees from fifty to seventy-five feet from the ground. Only two to four eggs are laid; these are whitish spotted with brown. These hawks are said to remain mated for life and are devoted to each other and their young. Hawks and eagles are very similar in form and habits, and if the eagle is a noble bird so is the hawk.

Northern harrier chicks

Lesson

Leading thought— Ignorant people consider all hawks dangerous neighbors because they are supposed to feed exclusively on poultry. This idea is false and we should study carefully the habits of hawks before we shoot them. The ordinary large reddish "hen-hawks," which circle high above meadows, are doing great good to the farmer by feeding upon the mice and other creatures which steal his grain and girdle his trees.

Methods— Begin by observations on the flight of one of these hawks and supplement this with such observations as the pupils are able to make, or facts which they can discover by talking with hunters or others and by reading.

Observations—

1. How can you tell a hawk, when flying, from a crow or other large bird? Describe how it soars. Does it move off in any direction; if so, does it move off in circles? How often does it make strokes with its

153

wings? Does it rise when it is facing the wind and fall as it turns its back to the wind?

2. Have you seen a hawk flap its wings many times and then soar for a time? If so, what hawk do you think it was? How does it differ in habits from the "hen-hawks?"

3. Have you noticed a hawk when soaring drop suddenly to earth? If so, why did it do this?

4. How does a hawk hunt? How can it see a mouse in a meadow when it is so high in the air that it looks like a circling speck in the sky? If it is so far-sighted as this, how can it be near-sighted enough to catch the mouse when it is close to it? Would you not have to use field glasses or telescope to do this?

5. When a hawk alights what sort of a place does it choose? How does it act?

6. Do hawks seize their prey with their claws or their beaks? What sort of feet and claws has the hawk? Describe the beak. What do you think this shaped beak is meant for?

7. Why do people shoot hawks? Why is it a sign of ignorance in people to wish to shoot all hawks?

8. What is the food of the red-shouldered hawk as shown by the bulletin of the U. S. Department of Agriculture or by the Audubon leaflets?

9. Where does the hawk place its nest? Of what does it build its nest?

10. Compare the food and the nesting habits of the red-shouldered and red-tailed hawks?

11. How devoted are the hawks to their mates and their young? Does a hawk, losing its mate, live alone ever after?

12. Describe the colors of the hen hawks and describe how you can tell the two species apart by the colors and markings of the tail.

13. What is the cry of the hawk? How can you tell the two species apart by this cry? Does the hawk give its cry only when on the wing?

14. Why should an eagle be considered so noble a bird and the hawk be so scorned? What difference is there between them in habits?

Osprey fledgling

Supplementary reading— *Audubon Educational Leaflets* Nos. 8, 9 and 10; "The Sparrow Hawk," *Familiar Wild Animals*, Lottridge; "Eyes and Cameras," also pp. 101-102, *The Bird Book*, Eckstorm; *Birds that Hunt and are Hunted*, pp. 317-319, 326, Blanchan; "Cloud Wings, The Eagle," in *Wilderness Ways*; "The Sky King and His Family," "Hannah Lomond's Bairn," in *Neighbors with Wings and Fins*; *American Birds*, Finley.

Reference books— *The Bird*, Beebe, pp. 389, 376, 208-211; *Hawks and Owls from the Standpoint of the Farmer*, Fisher, U. S. Department of Agriculture.

> *Yet, ere the noon, as brass the heaven turns,*
> *The cruel sun smites with unerring aim,*
> *The sight and touch of all things blinds and burns,*
> *And bare, hot hills seem shimmering into flame!*
>
> *On outspread wings a hawk, far poised on high,*
> *Quick swooping screams, and then is heard no more:*
> *The strident shrilling of a locust nigh*
> *Breaks forth, and dies in silence as before.*
>
> —"Summer Drought," by J. P. Irvine.

A wire-tailed swallow feeding a recently fledged chick

The Swallows and the Chimney Swift

TEACHER'S STORY

THESE friendly little birds spend their time darting through the air on swift wings, seeking and destroying insects which are foes to us and our various crops. However, it is safe to assume that they are not thinking of us as they skim above our meadows and ponds, hawking our tiny foes; for like most of us, they are simply intent upon getting a living. Would that we might perform this necessary duty as gracefully as they.

In general, the swallows have a long, slender, graceful body, with a long tail which is forked or notched, except in the case of the eave swallow. The beak is short but wide where it joins the head; this enables the bird to open its mouth wide and gives it more scope in the matter of catching insects; the swift flight of the swallows enables them to catch insects on the wing; their legs are short, the feet are weak and fitted for perching; it would be quite impossible for a swallow to walk or hop like a robin or blackbird.

The eave, or cliff, swallows— These swallows build under the eaves of barns or in similar locations. In early times they built against the sides of cliffs; but when man came and built barns, they chose them for their dwelling sites. The nest is made of mud pellets and is somewhat

156

globular in shape, with an entrance at one side. When building on the sides of cliffs or in unprotected portions of a barn, a covered passage is built around the door, which gives the nest the shape of a gourd or retort; but when protected beneath the eaves the birds seem to think this vestibule is unnecessary. The mud nest is warmly lined with feathers and soft materials, and there are often many nests built so closely together that they

A cliff swallow on its nest

touch. The eave swallow comes north about May 1st, and soon after that, may be seen along streams or other damp places gathering mud for the nests. It seems necessary for the bird to find clay mud in order to render the nest strong enough to support the eggs and nestlings. The eggs are white, blotched with reddish brown. The parents cling to the edge of the nest when feeding the young. Both the barn and eave swallows are blue above but the eave swallow has the forehead cream white and the rump of pale brick-red, and its tail is square across the end as seen in flight. The barn swallow has a chestnut forehead and its outer tail feathers are long, making a distinct fork during flight, and it is not red upon the rump.

The barn swallows— These birds choose a barn where there is a hole in the gable or where the doors are kept open all the time. They build upon beams or rafters, making a cup-shaped nest of layers of pellets of mud, with grass between; it is well lined with feathers. The nest is usually the shape of half of a shallow cup which has been cut in two lengthwise, the cut side being plastered against the side of the rafter. Sometimes the nests are more or less supported upon a beam or rafter; the eggs are white and dotted with reddish brown. The barn swallows, aside from their constant twittering, have also a pretty song.

Both parents work at building the nest and feeding the young; there are likely to be several pairs nesting in the same building. The parents continue to feed the young long after they have left the nest; often a whole family may be seen sitting on a telegraph wire or wire fence, the parents still feeding the well-grown youngsters. This species comes north in the latter part of April and leaves early in September. It winters as far south as Brazil.

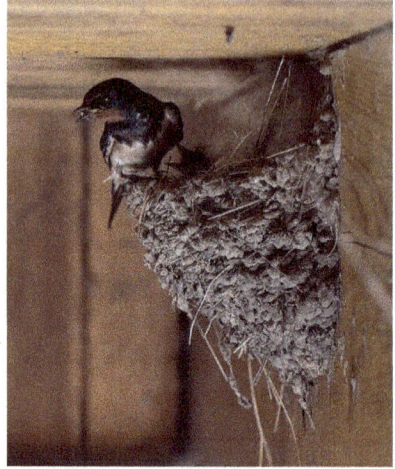

Barn swallow and nest

The barn swallow has a distinctly tailor-made appearance; its red-brown vest and iridescent blue coat, with deeply forked "coat tails" give it an elegance of style which no other bird, not even the chic cedar waxwing can emulate.

The Bank Swallow— When we see a sandy bank apparently shot full of holes as by small cannon balls, we may know that we have found a tenement of bank swallows. These birds always choose the perpendicular banks of creeks or of railroad cuts or of sand pits for their nesting sites; they require a soil sufficiently soft to be tunneled by their weak feet, and yet not so loose as to cave in upon the nest. The tunnel may extend from one to four feet horizontally in the bank with just enough diameter to admit the body of the rather small bird. The nest is situated at the extreme end of the tunnel and is lined with soft feathers and grasses.

Juvenile bank swallow

The bank swallows arrive late in April and leave early in September. They may be distinguished from the other species by their grayish color above; the throat and breast are white with a broad, brownish band across the breast; the tail is slightly forked. The rough-winged swallow, which is similar in habits to the bank swallow, may be distinguished from it by its gray breast, which has no dark band.

The Tree Swallow— This graceful little bird builds naturally in holes in trees, but readily accepts a box if it is provided. It begins to build soon after it comes north in late April and it is well for us to encourage the tree swallows to live near our houses by building houses for them and driving away the English sparrows. The tree swallows live upon many insects which annoy us and injure our gardens and damage our orchards; they are, therefore, much more desirable neighbors than the English sparrows. The tree swallows congregate in great numbers for the southern migration very early in the season, often in

Tree swallow

early August. They are likely to congregate in marshes, as are also the other swallows. In color the tree swallow has a green metallic back and head, a pure white breast with no band across it, and these peculiarities distinguish it from all other species.

The Purple Martin— The martin is a larger bird than the largest swallow, being eight inches in length, while the barn swallow does not measure quite seven. The male is shining, steel-blue above and below; the female is brownish above, has a gray throat, brownish breast and

A purple martin pair at nest site (the female is on the left)

is white beneath. The martins originally nested in hollow trees, but for centuries have been cared for by man. The Indians were wont to put out empty gourds for them to nest in; and as soon as America was settled by Europeans, martin boxes were built extensively. But when the English sparrows came, they took possession of the boxes, and the martins have to a large extent disappeared; this is a pity, since they are beneficial birds, feeding upon insects which are injurious to our farms and gardens. They are also delightful birds to have around, and we may possibly induce them to come back to us by building houses for them and driving away the sparrows.

THE CHIMNEY SWIFT

WHEN the old-fashioned fire-places went out of use and were walled up, leaving the great old chimneys useless, these sociable birds took possession of them. Here they built their nests and reared their young, and twittered and scrambled about, awakening all sleepers in the neighborhood at earliest dawn, and in many ways made themselves a distinct part of family life. With the disappearance of these old chimneys and the growing use of the smaller chimney, the swifts have been more or less driven from their close association with people; and now their nests are often found in hay barns or other secluded buildings, although they still gather in chimneys when opportunity offers.

The chimney swifts originally built nests in hollow trees and caves; but with the coming of civilization they took possession of the chim-

A chimney of swifts!

neys disused during the summer, and here is where we know them best. The nests are shaped like little wall pockets; they are made of small sticks of nearly uniform size which are glued together and glued fast to the chimney wall by means of the saliva secreted in the mouth of the bird. After the nesting season, the swifts often gather in great flocks and live together in some large chimney; toward night-fall they may be seen circling about in great numbers and dropping into the mouth of the chimney, one by one, as if they were being poured into a funnel. In the morning they leave in reverse manner, each swift flying about in widening circles as it leaves the chimney. The swifts are never seen to alight anywhere except in hollow trees or chimneys or similar places; their tiny feet have sharp claws for clinging to the slightest roughness of the upright wall; the tail acts as a prop, each tail feather ending in a spine which is pressed against the chimney side when the bird alights and thus enables it to cling more firmly. In this fashion the swifts roost, practically hung up against a wall.

The swift has a short beak and wide mouth which it opens broadly to engulf insects as it darts through the air. Chimney swifts have been known to travel at the rate of 110 miles an hour.

This bird should never be confused with the swallows, for when flying, its tail seems simply a sharp point, making the whole body cigar-shaped. This character alone distinguishes it from the long tailed swallows. In color it is sooty brown, with a gray throat and breast; the wings are long and narrow and apparently curved. The manner of flight and appearance in the air make it resemble the bat more than it does the swallow.

LESSON

Leading thought— The swallows are very graceful birds and are exceedingly swift fliers. They feed upon insects which they catch upon the wing. There are five native swallows which are common—the eave, or cliff, the barn, the bank, the tree swallow and the purple martin. The chimney swift, although often called so, is not a swallow; it is more nearly related to the hummingbird than to the swallows.

Method— The questions should be given as an outline for observation, and may be written on the blackboard or placed in the field notebook. The pupils should answer them individually and from field observation. We study the swifts and swallows together to teach the pupils to distinguish them apart.

Observations—

1. What is the general shape of the swallow? What is the color of the forehead, throat, upper breast, neck, rump and tail?

2. Is the tail noticeably forked especially during flight?

3. Describe the flight of the swallow. What is the purpose of its long, swift flight? How are the swallow's wings fitted for carrying the bird swiftly?

4. Describe the form of the beak of the swallow. How does it get its food? What is its food?

5. In what particular locations do you see the swallows darting about? At what time of day do they seem most active?

6. Describe the swallow's legs and feet and explain why they look so different from those of the robin and blackbird.

Young barn swallows. Notice the feathers lining the nest

THE EAVE, OR CLIFF SWALLOW

7. Where do the eave swallows build their nests? Of what material is the outside? The lining? Describe the shape of the nest and how it is supported.

8. How early in the spring do the eave swallows begin to make their nests? Where and by what means do they get the material for nest building? Are there a number of nests usually grouped together?

9. Describe the eave swallow's egg. Where do the parents sit when feeding the young? What is the note of the eave swallow?

10. What are the differences between the barn and the eave swallow in color and shape of tail?

THE BARN SWALLOW

11. Where does the barn swallow place its nest? What is the shape of the nest? Of what material is it made?

12. What is the color of the eggs? Describe the feeding of the young and the sounds made by them and their parents. Do both parents work together to build the nest and feed the young?

13. Is there usually more than one nest in the same locality? When the young swallows are large enough to leave the nest, describe how the parents continue to care for them.

14. Have you ever heard the barn swallows sing? Describe their conversational notes.

15. When do the barn swallows migrate and where do they go during the winter? How can you distinguish the barn swallow from the eave swallow?

Swallow nests on a cliff

THE BANK SWALLOW

16. Where do the bank swallows build? What sort of soil do they choose?

17. How does a bank look which is tenanted by these birds?

18. How far do the bank swallows tunnel into the earth? What is the diameter of one of these tunnels? Do they extend straight or do they rise or deflect?

19. With what tools is the tunnel excavated? Where is the nest situated in the tunnel and how is it lined?

20. How can you distinguish this species from the barn and eave and tree swallows? At what time do the bank swallows leave us for migration south?

THE TREE SWALLOW

21. Where does the tree swallow make its nest? How does its nest differ from that of the barn, eave, or bank swallow? When does it begin to build?

22. How can we encourage the tree swallow to build near our houses? Why is the tree swallow a much more desirable bird to have in bird houses than the English sparrow?

23. Describe the peculiar migrating habits of the tree swallow. How can you tell this species from the barn, the eave and the bank swallows?

THE PURPLE MARTIN

24. Compare the purple martin with the swallows and describe how it differs in size and color.

25. Where did the martins build their nests before America was civilized? Where do they like to nest now? How do the purple martins benefit us and how can we induce them to come to us?

THE CHIMNEY SWIFT

26. Where do the chimney swifts build their nests? Of what materials is the nest made? What is its shape

KEWLGRAPES (CC BY-SA 4.0)
Tree swallow nest

and how is it supported? Where does the chimney swift get its glue for nest building?

27. Describe how the chimney swifts enter their nesting place at night. Where and how do they perch? Describe the shape of the swift's tail and its use to the bird when roosting.

28. On what does the chimney swift feed and how does it procure this food? Describe how its beak is especially fitted for this?

29. How can you distinguish the chimney swift from the swallows? In what respect does the chimney swift resemble the swallows? In what respects does it differ from them?

Supplementary reading— "Chimney Swifts," *Familiar Wild Animals*, Lottridge; *The Chimney Swifts*, Washington Irving; *Nestlings of Forest and Marsh*, Wheelock, p. 191; "The Eave Swallow" and "The Purple Martin" in *The Bird Book*, Eckstorm; *The Second Bird Book*, Miller; *True Bird Stories*, Miller, p. 118; *Our Birds and Their Nestlings*, p. 155; *A Watcher in the Woods*, Sharp, p. 163.

The Hummingbird

TEACHER'S STORY

FORMERLY it was believed that this daintiest of birds found the nectar of flowers ample support for its active life; but the later methods of discovering what birds eat by examining the contents of their stomachs, show that the hummingbird is an insect eater of most ravenous appetite. Not only does it catch insects in mid air, but undoubtedly takes them while they are feasting on the nectar of the tubular flowers which the hummingbird loves to visit. Incidentally, the hummingbird carries the pollen for these flowers and may be counted as a friend in every respect, since usually the insects in the nectaries of the flowers with long tubular corollas, are stealing nectar without giving in return compensation to the flower by carrying its pollen. Such insects may be the smaller beetles, ants and flies. The adaptations of the hummingbird's beak and long, double-tubed tongue, are especially for securing this mingled diet of insects and nectar. It is interesting to note that the young hummingbirds have the beak much shorter than when mature. Its beak is exactly fitted to probe those flowers where the hummingbird finds its food. The tongue has the outer edges curved over making a tube on each side. These tubes are provided with minute brushes at the tips and thus are fitted both for sucking nectar and for sweeping up the insects.

A hummingbird feeds insects to her nestlings

The natural home of the hummingbird seems to have been in the American tropics. Our one species east of the Rocky Mountains with which we are all familiar has a ruby throat. This comes to us after a very long journey each year. One species on the Pacific Coast is known to travel three thousand miles to the north for the summer and back again in winter.

Hummingbirds are not supposed to sing, but to use their voices for squeaking when angry or frightened. However, I once had the privilege of listening to a true song by a hummingbird on the Pacific Coast. The midget was perched upon a twig and lifted up his voice with every appearance of ecstasy in pouring forth his lay. To my uncultured ear this song was a fine, shrill, erratic succession of squeaks, "as fine as a cambric needle," said my companion.

The nest of the hummingbird is a most exquisite structure; it is about three-fourths of an inch in diameter on the inside and about half an inch deep. It is, in shape, a symmetrical cup; the outside is covered with lichens to make it exactly resemble the branch on which it rests; the inside is lined with the down of plant seeds and plant fibres. The lichens are often fastened to the outside with the silk web of spiders or caterpillars. The nest is usually saddled on a branch of a tree

Looking like a knot on a branch, the hummingbird nest is not much bigger than a walnut

from 10 to 50 feet above the ground. The eggs are two in number and white; they look like tiny beans. The young are black and look, at first glance, more like insects than like birds.

LESSON

Leading thought— The hummingbird in flight moves its wings so rapidly that we cannot see them. It can hold itself poised above flowers while it thrusts its long beak into them for nectar and insects.

Method— Give the questions to the pupils and let them make the observations when they have the opportunity.

Observations—

1. Where do you find the hummingbird? What flowers was it visiting? At what time of day? Can you tell whether it is a hummingbird or a hawk-moth which is visiting the flowers? At what time of day do the hawk-moths appear?

2. Does the hummingbird ever come to rest? Describe its actions while resting.

3. What are the colors of the back, throat, breast and under parts? How do you distinguish the mother hummingbird from her mate?

4. How does the hummingbird act when extracting the nectar? How does it balance itself in front of a flower? Have you ever seen hummingbirds catch insects in the air? If so, describe how they did it.

5. Describe the hummingbird's nest. How large is it in diameter? What is the covering outside? With what is it lined?

The Red-Winged Blackbird

TEACHER'S STORY

THE blackbirds are among our earliest visitors in the spring; they come in flocks and beset our leafless trees like punctuation marks, meanwhile squeaking like musical wheelbarrows. What they are, where they come from, where they are going and what they are going to do, are the questions that naturally arise at the sight of these sable flocks. It is not easy to distinguish grackles, cowbirds and rusty blackbirds at a glance, but the red-wing proclaims his identity from afar. The bright red epaulets, margined behind with pale yellow, is a uniform to catch the admiring eye. The bird's glossy black plumage brings into greater contrast his bright decorations. That he is fully aware of his beauty, who can doubt who has seen him come sailing down at the end of his strong, swift flight, and balancing himself on some bending reed, drop his long tail as if it were the crank of his music box, and holding both wings lifted to show his scarlet decorations, sing his "quong quer ee-ee." Little wonder that such a handsome, military looking fellow should be able now and then to win more than his share of feminine admiration. But what though he become an entirely successful bigamist or even trigamist, he has proven himself to be a good protector of each and all of his wives and nestlings; however, he often has but one mate.

The nest and eggs of a red-winged blackbird

The nest is now getting quite full. The young are in the nest for about two weeks

"The red-wing flutes his O-ka-lee" is Emerson's graphic description of the sweet song of the red-wing; he also has many other notes. He clucks to his mates and clucks more sharply when suspicious, and has one alarm note that is truly alarming. The male red-wings come from the South in March; they appear in flocks, often three weeks before their mates arrive. The female looks as though she belonged to quite a different species. Although her head and back are black, the black is decidedly rusty; it is quite impossible to describe her, she is so inconspicuously speckled with brown, black, whitish buff and orange. Most of us never recognize her unless we see her with her spouse. As she probably does most of the nest building, her suit of salt, pepper and mustard renders her invisible to the keen eyes of birds of prey. Only when she is flying, does she show her blackbird characteristics,—her tail being long and of obvious use as a steering organ; and she walks with long, stiff strides. The red-wings are ever to be found in and about swamps and marshes. The nest is built usually in May; it is made of grasses, stalks of weeds and is lined with finer grass or reeds. It is bulky and is placed in low bushes or among the reeds. The eggs are pale blue, streaked and spotted with purple or black. The young resemble the mother in color, the males being obliged to wait a year for their epaulets. As to the food of the red-wings here in the North, Mr. Forbush says:

"Although the red-wings almost invariably breed in the swamp or marsh, they have a partiality for open fields and plowed lands; however, most of the blackbirds that nest in the smaller swamps adjacent to farm lands get a large share of their food from the farmer's fields. They forage about the fields and meadows when they first come north in the spring. Later, they follow the plow, picking up grubs, worms and caterpillars; and should there be an outbreak of canker-worms in the orchard, the blackbirds will fly at least half a mile to get canker-worms for their young. Wilson estimated that the red-wings of the United States would in four months destroy sixteen thousand two hundred million larvae. They eat the caterpillars of the gypsy moth, the forest tent-caterpillar, and other hairy larvae. They are among the most destructive birds to weevils, click beetles, and wire-worms. Grasshoppers, ants, bugs, and flies form a portion of the red-wing's food. They eat comparatively little grain in Massachusetts, although they get some from newly sown fields in spring, as well as from the autumn harvest; but they feed very largely on the seeds of weeds and wild rice in the fall. In the South they join with the bobolink in devastating the rice fields, and in the West they are often so numerous as to destroy the grain in the fields; but here the good they do far outweighs the injury, and for this reason they are protected by law."

Lesson

Leading thought— The red-winged blackbird lives in the marshes where it builds its nest. However, it comes over to our plowed lands and pastures and helps the farmer by destroying many insects which injure the meadows, crops and trees.

Method— The observations should be made by the pupils individually in the field. These birds may be looked for in flocks early in the spring, but the study should be made in May or June when they will be found in numbers in almost any swamp. The questions may be given to the pupils a few at a time or written in their field notebooks and the answers discussed when discovered.

Observations—

1. How can you distinguish the red-winged blackbird from all other blackbirds? Where is the red on his wings? Is there any other color besides red on the wings? Where? What is the color of the rest of the plumage?

2. What is there peculiar in the flight of the red-wing? Is its tail long or short? How does it use its tail in flight? What is its position when the bird alights on a reed?

3. What is the song of the red-wing? Describe the way he holds his wings and tail when singing, balanced on a reed or some other swamp grass. Does he show off his epaulets when singing? Why? What note does he give when he is surprised or suspicious? When frightened?

4. When does the red-wing first appear in the spring? Does he come alone or in flocks? Does his mate come with him? Where do the red-wings winter? In what localities do the red-wing blackbirds live? Why do they live there? What is the color of the mother red-wing? Would you know by her looks that she was a blackbird? What advantage is it to the pair that the female is so dull in color?

5. At what time do these birds nest? Where is the nest built? Of what material? How is it concealed? What is the color of the eggs?

6. Do the young birds resemble in color their father or their mother? Why is this an advantage?

7. Is the red-wing ever seen in fields adjoining the marshes? What is he doing there? Does he walk or hop when looking for food? What is the food of the red-wings? Do they ever damage grain? Do they not protect grain more than they damage it?

8. What great good do the red-wings do for forest trees? For orchards?

9. At what time in the summer do the red-wings disappear from the swamps? Where do they gather in flocks? Where is their special feeding ground on the way south for the winter?

The Baltimore Oriole

TEACHER'S STORY

"I know his name, I know his note,
  That so with rapture takes my soul;
Like flame the gold beneath his throat,
  His glossy cope is black as coal.
O Oriole, it is the song
  You sang me from the cottonwood,
Too young to feel that I was young,
  Too glad to guess if life were good."

—WILLIAM DEAN HOWELLS.

DANGLING from the slender, drooping branches of the elm in winter, these pocket nests look like some strange persistent fruit; and, indeed, they are the fruit of much labor on the part of the oriole weavers, those skilled artisans of the bird world. Sometimes the oriole "For the summer voyage his hammock swings" in a sapling, placing it near the main stem and near the top, otherwise it is almost invariably hung at the end of branches and is rarely less than twenty feet

An oriole's nest woven into the leaves of a tree

from the ground. The nest is pocket-shaped, and usually about seven inches long, and four and a half inches wide at the largest part, which is the bottom. The top is attached to forked twigs at the Y so that the mouth or door will be kept open to allow the bird to pass in and out; when within, the weight of the bird causes the opening to contract somewhat and protects the inmate from prying eyes. Often the pocket hangs free so that the breezes may rock it, but in one case we found a nest with the bottom stayed to a twig by guy lines. The bottom is much more closely woven than the upper part for a very good reason, since the open meshes admit air to the sitting bird. The nest is lined with hair or other soft material, and although this is added last, the inside of the nest is woven first. The orioles like to build the framework of twine, and it is marvellous how they will loop this around a twig almost as evenly knotted as if crocheted; in and out of this net the mother bird with her long, sharp beak weaves bits of wood fibre, strong, fine grass and scraps of weeds. The favorite lining is horse hair, which simply cushions the bottom of the pocket. Dr. Detwiler had a pet oriole which built her nest of his hair which she pulled from his head; is it possible that orioles get their supply of horse hair in a similar way?

174

If we put in convenient places, bright colored twine or narrow ribbons the orioles will weave them into the nest, but the strings should not be long, lest the birds become entangled. If the nest is strong the birds will use it a second year.

That Lord Baltimore found in new America a bird wearing his colors, must have cheered him greatly; and it is well for us that this brilliant bird brings to our minds kindly thoughts of that tolerant, high-minded English nobleman. The oriole's head, neck, throat and part of the back are black; the wings are black but the feathers are margined with white; the tail is black except that the ends of the outer feathers are yellow; all the rest of the bird is golden orange, a luminous color which makes him seem a splash of brilliant sunshine. The female, although marked much the same, has the back so dull and mottled that it looks olive-brown; the rump, breast, and under parts are yellow but by no means showy. The advantage of these quiet colors to the mother bird is obvious since it is she that makes the nest and sits in it without attracting attention to its location. In fact, when she is sitting, her brilliant mate places himself far enough away to distract the attention of meddlers, yet near enough for her to see the flash of his breast in the sunshine and to hear his rich and cheering song. He is a good spouse and brings her the materials for the nest which she weaves in, hanging head downward from a twig and using her long sharp beak for a shuttle. And his glorious song is for her alone; some hold that no two orioles have the same song; I know of two individuals at least whose songs were sung by no other birds; one gave a phrase from the Waldvogel's song in Sigfried; the other whistled over and over, "Sweet birdie, hello, hello." The orioles can chatter and scold as well as sing.

The oriole is a brave defender of his nest and a most devoted father, working hard to feed his ever hungry nestlings; we can hear these hollow mites peeping for more food, "Tee dee dee, Tee dee dee", shrill and constant, if we stop for a moment under the nest in June. The young birds dress in the safe colors of the mother, the males not donning their bright plumage until the second year. A brilliant colored fledgling would not live long in a world where sharp eyes are in constant quest for little birds to fill empty stomachs.

The food of the oriole places it among our most beneficial birds,

An orchard oriole

since it is always ready to cope with the hairy caterpillars avoided by most birds; it has learned to abstract the caterpillar from his spines and is thus able to swallow him minus his "whiskers." The orioles are waging a great war against the terrible brown-tail and gipsy moths in New England; they also eat click beetles and many other noxious insects. Once when we were breeding big caterpillars in the Cornell insectary, an oriole came in through the open windows of the greenhouse, and, thinking he had found a bonanza, proceeded to work it, carrying off our precious crawlers before we discovered what he was at.

The orioles winter in Central America and give us scarcely four months of their company. They do not usually appear before May and leave in early September.

LESSON

Leading thought— The oriole is the most skillful of all our bird architects. It is also one of our prized song birds and is very beneficial to the farmer and fruit grower because of the insect pests which it destroys.

Method— Begin during winter or early spring with a study of the nest, which may be obtained from the elms of the roadsides. During the first week in May, give the questions concerning the birds and their habits. Let the pupils keep the questions in their note-books and answer them when they have opportunity. The observations should be summed up once a week.

Observations by pupils—

1. Where did you find the nest? On what species of tree? Was it near the trunk of the tree or the tip of the branch?

2. What is the shape of the nest? How long is it? How wide? Is the opening as large as the bottom of the nest? How is it hung to the twigs so that the opening remains open and does not pull together with the weight of the bird at the bottom? Is the bottom of the nest stayed to a twig or does it hang loose?

3. With what material and how is the nest fastened to the branches? Of what material is the outside made? How is it woven together? Is it more loosely woven at the top than at the bottom? How many kinds of material can you find in the outside of the nest?

4. With what is the nest lined? How far up is it lined? With what tool was the nest woven? If you put out bright colored bits of ribbon and string do you think the orioles will use them? Why should you not put out long strings?

5. At what date did you first see the Baltimore oriole? Why is it called the Baltimore oriole? How many other names has it? Describe in the following way the colors of the male oriole: top of head, back, wings, tail, throat, breast, under parts. What are the colors of his mate? How would it endanger the nest and nestlings if the mother bird were as bright colored as the father bird?

6. Which weaves the nest, the father or the mother bird? Does the former assist in any way in nest building?

7. Where does the father bird stay and what does he do while the mother bird is sitting on the eggs?

8. What is the oriole's song? Has he more than one song? What other notes has he? After the young birds hatch does the father bird help take care of them?

9. By the middle of June the young birds are usually hatched and if

Baby oriole feeding

you know where an oriole nest is hung, listen and describe the call of the nestlings for food.

10. Which parent do the young birds resemble in their colors? Why is this a benefit?

11. What is the oriole's food? How is the oriole of benefit to us in ways which other birds are not?

12. Do the orioles use the same nest two years in succession? How long does the oriole stay in the North? Where does it spend its winters?

> "Hush! 'tis he!
> My oriole, my glance of summer fire,
> Is come at last, and, ever on the watch,
> Twitches the packthread I had lightly wound
> About the bough to help his housekeeping,—
> Twitches and scouts by turns, blessing his luck,
> Yet fearing me who laid it in his way,
> Nor, more than wiser we in our affairs.
> Divines the Providence that hides and helps.
> Heave, ho! Heave, ho! he whistles as the twine
> Slackens its hold; once more, now! and a flash
> Lightens across the sunlight to the elm
> Where his mate dangles at her cup of felt."
>
> —"UNDER THE WILLOWS", LOWELL.

The Crow

Teacher's Story

THOREAU says: "What a perfectly New England sound is this voice of the crow! If you stand still anywhere in the outskirts of the town and listen, this is perhaps the sound which you will be most sure to hear, rising above all sounds of human industry and leading your thoughts to some far-away bay in the woods. The bird sees the white man come and the Indian withdraw, but it withdraws not. Its untamed voice is still heard above the tinkling of the forge. It sees a race pass away, but it passes not away. It remains to remind us of aboriginal nature."

The crow is probably the most intelligent of all our native birds. It is quick to learn and clever in action, as many a farmer will testify who has tried to keep it out of corn fields with various devices, the harmless character of which the crow soon understood perfectly. Of all our birds, this one has the longest list of virtues and of sins, as judged from our standpoint; but we should listen to both sides of the case before we pass judgment. I find with crows, as with people, I like some more than I do others. I do not like at all the cunning old crow which steals the suet I put on the trees in winter for the chickadees and nuthatches; and I have hired a boy with a shotgun to protect the

Crow nests in a tree

eggs and nestlings of the robins and other birds in my neighborhood from the ravages of one or two cruel old crows that have developed the nest-hunting habit. On the other hand, I became a sincere admirer of a crow flock which worked in a field close to my country home, and I have been the chosen friend of several tame crows who were even more interesting than they were mischievous.

The crow is larger than any other of our common blackbirds; the northern raven is still larger, but is very rarely seen. Although the crow's feathers are black, yet in the sunlight a beautiful purple iridescence plays over the plumage, especially about the neck and back; it has a compact but not ungraceful body, and long, powerful wings; its tail is medium sized and is not notched at the end; its feet are long and strong; the track shows three toes directed forward and one long one directed backward. The crow does not sail through the air as does the hawk, but progresses with an almost constant flapping of the wings. Its beak is very strong and is used for tearing the flesh of its prey and for defense, and in fact, for almost anything that a beak could be used for; its eye is all black and is very keen and intelligent. When hunting for food in the field, it usually walks, but sometimes hops. The raven and the fish crows are the nearest relatives of the American crow, and next to them the jays. We should hardly think that the bluejay and the crow were related to look at them, but when we come to study their habits, much is to be found in common.

The crow's nest is usually very large; it is made of sticks, of grape vines and bark, sod, horse-hair, moss and grasses. It is placed in trees or in tall bushes rarely less than twenty feet from the ground. The eggs are pale bluish green or nearly white with brownish markings. The young crows hatch in April or May. Both parents are devoted to the care of the young, and remain with them during most of the summer. I have often seen a mother crow feeding her young ones which were following her with obstreperous caws, although they were as large as she.

While the note of the crow is harsh when close at hand, it has a musical quality in the distance. Mr. Mathews says: "The crow when he sings is nothing short of a clown; he ruffles his feathers, stretches his neck, like a cat with a fish bone in her throat, and with a most tremendous effort delivers a series of hen-like squawks." But aside from his caw, the crow has some very seductive soft notes. I have held long conversations with two pet crows, talking with them in a high, soft tone and finding that they answered readily in a like tone in a most responsive way. I have also heard these same tones among the wild crows when they were talking together; one note is a gutteral tremolo, most grotesque.

Crows gather in flocks for the winter; these flocks number from fifty to several hundred individuals, all having a common roosting place, usually in pine or hemlock forests or among other evergreens. They go out from these roosts during the day to get food, often making a journey of many miles. During the nesting season they scatter in pairs and do not gather again in flocks until the young are fully grown.

When crows are feeding in the fields there is usually, if not always, a sentinel posted on some high point so that he can give warning of danger. This sentinel is always an experienced bird and is keen to detect a dangerous from a harmless intruder. I once made many experiments with these sentinels; I finally became known to those of a particular flock and I was allowed to approach within a few yards of where the birds were feeding, a privilege not accorded to any other person in the neighborhood.

The crow is a general feeder and will eat almost any food; gener-

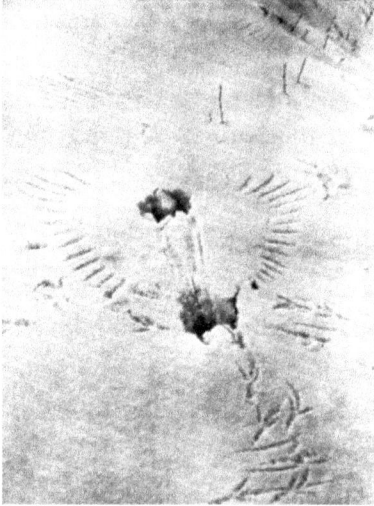
The story of a take-off. With the third wing beat the crow is away

ally, however, it finds its food upon the ground. The food given to nestlings is very largely insects, and many pests are thus destroyed. The crows damage the farmer by pulling the sprouting corn and by destroying the eggs and young of poultry. They also do much harm by destroying the eggs and nestlings of our native birds which are beneficial to the farmer; they also do some harm by distributing the seeds of poison ivy and other noxious plants. All these must be set down in the account against the crow, but on the credit side must be placed the fact that it does a tremendous amount of good work for the farmer by eating injurious insects, especially the grubs and cut-worms which work in the ground, destroying the roots of grasses and grains. It also kills many mice and other rodents which are destructive to crops.

The best method of preventing crows from taking sprouting corn is to tar the seed corn, which is planted around the edge of the field.

If any of the pupils in your school have had any experience with tame crows they will relate interesting incidents of the love of the crow for glittering objects. I once knew a tame crow which stole all of the thimbles in the house and buried them in the garden; he would watch to see when a thimble was laid aside when the sewing was dropped, and would seize it almost immediately. This same crow persisted in taking the clothespins off the line and burying them, so that he was finally imprisoned on wash-days. He was fond of playing marbles with a little boy of the family. The boy would shoot a marble into a hole and then Billy, the crow, would take a marble in his beak and drop it into the hole. The bird understood the game perfectly and was highly indignant if the boy took his turn and made shots twice in succession.

References— *The American Crow*, Barrows & Schwartz, Bulletin No. 6, Division of Ornithology, U. S. Department of Agriculture; *Birds in Relation to Man*, Weed & Dearborn; *Bird Neighbors*, Blanchan; *Birds of Villages and Field*, Merriam; *Outdoor Studies*, Needham.

Ingrid Taylar (cc by 2.0)

American crow and fledgling. Notice the grey-blue eyes of the young crow which turn dark brown as they get older

Lesson

Leading thought— The crow has the keenest intelligence of any of our common birds. It does good work for us and also does damage. We should study its ways before we pronounce judgment, for in some localities it may be a true friend and in others an enemy.

Methods— This work should begin in winter with an effort on the part of the boys to discover the food of the crows while snow is on the ground. This is a good time to study their habits and their roosts. The nests are also often found in winter, although usually built in evergreens. The nesting season is in early April, and the questions about the nests should be given then. Let the other questions be given when convenient. The flight, the notes, the sentinels, the food, the benefit and damage may all be taken as separate topics.

The following topics for essays should be given to correlate with work in English: "What a pet crow of my acquaintance did;" "Evidences of crow intelligence;" "A plea a crow might make in self-defence to the farmer who wished to shoot him;" "The best methods of preventing crows from stealing planted corn."

Observations—

1. How large is the crow compared with other blackbirds?
2. Describe its colors when seen in the sunlight.
3. Describe the general shape of the crow.
4. Are its wings long and slender or short and stout?

183

5. Is the tail long or short? Is it notched or straight across the end?

6. Describe the crow's feet. Are they large and strong or slender? How many toes does the track show in the snow or mud? How many are directed forward and how many backward?

7. Describe a crow's flight compared with that of the hawk.

8. Describe its beak and what it is used for.

9. What is the color of the crow's eye?

10. When hunting for food does the crow hop or walk?

11. Which are the crow's nearest relatives?

12. Where and of what material do the crows build their nests?

13. Describe the eggs. At what time of the year do the young crows hatch? Do both parents take care of and feed the young? How long do the parents care for the young after they leave the nest?

14. What are the notes of the crow? If you have heard one give any note except "caw," describe it.

15. Where and how do crows live in winter? Where do they live in summer?

16. Do they post sentinels if they are feeding in the fields? If so, describe the action of the sentinel on the approach of people.

17. Upon what do the crows feed? What is fed to the nestlings?

18. How do the crows work injury to the farmer? How do they benefit the farmer? Do you think they do more benefit than harm to the farmer and fruit-grower?

19. Have you known of instances of the crow's fondness for shining or glittering articles, like pieces of crockery or tin?

Supplementary reading— "The Story of Silver Spot" in *Wild Animals I have Known*, Seton; *Second Book of Birds*, p. 117; "Jim's Babies" in *Nestlings of Forest and Marsh*; "How the Crow Baby was Punished," *True Bird Stories*; "The Children of a Crow," and "The Scare Crow" by Celia Thaxter; *Our Birds and their Nestlings*; "Crow Ways," *Ways of Wood Folk*, Long; "Not so Black as he is Painted," *Outdoor Studies*, Needham; *The Crows*, John Hay; "Jack Crow," *American Birds*, Finley.

The Cardinal Grosbeak

THERE never lived a Lord Cardinal who possessed robes of state more brilliant in color than the plumage of this bird. By the way, I wonder how many of us ever think when we see the peculiar red, called cardinal, that it gained its name from the dress of this high functionary of the church? The cardinal grosbeak is the best name for the redbird because that describes it exactly, both as to its color and its chief characteristic, since its beak is thick and large; the beak is also red, which is a rare color in beaks, and in order to make its redness more emphatic it is set in a frame of black feathers. The use of such a large beak is unmistakable, for it is strong enough to crush the hardest of seed shells or to crack the hardest and driest of grains.

> "What cheer! What cheer!
> That is the grosbeak's way,
> With his sooty face and his coat of red,"

sings Maurice Thompson. But besides the name given above, this bird has been called in different localities the redbird, Virginia redbird,

The cardinal builds its nest in thick bushes or vines.

crested redbird, winter redbird, Virginia nightingale, the red corn-cracker; but it remained for James Lane Allen to give it another name in his masterpiece, "The Kentucky Cardinal."

The cardinal is a trifle smaller than the robin and is by no means slim and graceful, like the catbird or the scarlet tanager, but is quite stout and is a veritable chunk of brilliant color and bird dignity. The only other bird that rivals him in redness is the scarlet tanager, which has black wings; the summer tanager is also a red bird, but is not so vermilion and is more slender and lacks the crest. The cardinal surely finds his crest useful in expressing his emotions; when all is serene, it lies back flat on the head, but with any excitement, whether of joy or surprise or anger, it lifts until it is as peaked as an old-fashioned nightcap. The cardinal's mate is of quiet color; her back is greenish gray and breast buffy, while her crest, wings and tail reflect in faint ways the brilliancy of his costume.

The redbird's song is a stirring succession of syllables uttered in a rich, ringing tone, and may be translated in a variety of ways. I have heard him sing a thousand times "tor-re'-do, tor-re'-do, tor-re'-do," but Dr. Dawson has heard him sing "che'-pew, che'-pew, we'-woo, we'-woo;" "bird-ie, bird-ie, bird-ie; tschew, tschew, tschew;" and "chit-e-kew, chit-e-kew; he-weet, he-weet." His mate breaks the custom of other birds of her sex and sings a sweet song, somewhat softer than his. Both birds utter a sharp note "tsip, tsip."

The nest is built in bushes, vines or low trees, often in holly, laurel or other low evergreens, and is rarely more than six or eight feet above the ground. It is made of twigs, weed stems, tendrils, the bark of the grape vine and coarse grass; it is lined with fine grass and rootlets; it is rather loosely constructed but firm and is well hidden, for it causes these birds great anguish to have their nest discovered. Three or four eggs are laid, which are bluish white or grayish, dully marked with brown. The father cardinal is an exemplary husband and father; he cares for and feeds his mate tenderly and sings to her gloriously while she is sitting; and he works hard catching insects for the nestlings. He is also a brave defender of his nest and will attack any intruder, however large, with undaunted courage. The fledglings all have the dull color of the mother and have dark-colored bills. Their dull color protects the young birds from the keen eyes of their enemies while they are not yet able to take care of themselves. If the male fledglings were the color of their father, probably not one would escape a tragic death. While the mother bird is hatching the second brood the father keeps the first brood with him and cares for them; often the whole family remains together during the winter, making a small flock. However, the flocking habit is not characteristic of these birds, and we only see them in considerable numbers when the exigencies of seeking food in the winter naturally bring them together.

The cardinals are fond of the shrubbery and thickets of river bottoms, near grain fields, or where there is plenty of wild grass, and they only visit our premises when driven to us by winter hunger. Their food consists of the seeds of rank weeds, corn, wheat, rye, oats, beetles, grasshoppers, flies, and to some extent, wild and garden berries; but they never occur in sufficient numbers to be a menace to our crops. The cardinals may often be seen in the corn fields after the harvest, and will husk an overlooked ear of corn and crack the kernels with their beaks in a most dexterous manner. During the winter we may coax them to our grounds by scattering corn in some place not frequented by cats; thus, we may induce them to nest near us, since the cardinal is not naturally a migrant but likes to stay in one locality summer and winter. It has been known to come as far north as Boston and southern New York, but it is found in greatest numbers in our Southern States. Many nestlings were formerly taken, to ship in cages to Europe, but the National Association for Bird Protection has put a stop to this. In Ohio, no cardinal is allowed to be caged, and this same

The cardinal sings a beautiful song

law should protect this beautiful bird in every Southern state, since it does not live long or happily in confinement. The cardinal's song is not at its best in a cage, but as the poet Naylor says:

> *"Along the dust-white river road,*
> *The saucy redbird chirps and trills;*
> *His liquid notes resound and rise*
> *Until they meet the cloudless skies,*
> *And echo o'er the distant hills."*

LESSON

Leading thought— The cardinal is the most brilliantly colored of all our birds and because of its color and song, it has been destroyed by thousands as cage birds. We should seek to preserve it as a beautiful ornament to our groves and grounds.

Methods— This work must be done by personal observation in the field. The field notes should be discussed in school. The effect of the whole lesson should be to stimulate an interest in protecting these beautiful birds. If possible, send for outline figures of the cardinal for the children to color; these outlines may be had at the cost of fifteen cents per dozen from the Audubon Society, 141 Broadway, New York City.

Observations—

1. Do you know the cardinal? Why is it so called?

2. How many names do you know for this bird?

3. Is the cardinal as large as the robin? Is it graceful in shape or stout?

4. Is there any color except red upon it? If so, where?

5. What other vividly red birds have we and how can we distinguish them from the cardinal?

6. Describe the cardinal's crest and how it looks when lifted. Why do you think it lifts it?

7. Describe its beak as to color, shape and size. What work is such a heavy beak made for?

8. Is the cardinal's mate the same color as he? Describe the color of her head, back, wings, tail, breast.

9. Can you imitate the cardinal's song? What words do you think he seems to sing? Does his mate sing also? Is it usual for mother birds to sing? What other notes besides songs do you hear him utter?

10. Where does the cardinal usually build its nest? How high from the ground? Of what materials? Is it compact or bulky? How many eggs and what are their colors?

11. How does the father bird act while his mate is brooding? How does he help take care of the young in the nest?

12. How do the fledglings differ in color from their father? From their mother? Of what use to the young birds is their sober color?

13. What happens to the fledglings of the first brood while the mother is hatching the eggs of the second brood?

14. In what localities do you most often see the cardinals? Do you ever see them in flocks?

15. What is the food of the cardinals? What do they feed their nestlings?

16. How can you induce the cardinals to build near your home?

17. What do you know about the laws protecting the redbirds?

Supplementary reading— The Second Book of Birds, Miller, p. 83; *True Bird Stories*, Miller, p. 86; *The Song of the Cardinal*, Porter; Audubon Educational Leaflet No. 18.

> *"Upon the gray old forest's rim*
> *I snuffed the crab-tree's sweet perfume;*
> *And farther, where the light was dim, I saw the bloom*
> *Of May apples, beneath the tent*
> *Of umbrel leaves above them bent,*
> *Where oft was shifting light and shade*
> *The blue-eyed ivy wildly strayed;*
> *The Solomon's seal, in graceful play,*
> *Swung where the straggling sunlight lay*
> *The same as when I earliest heard*
> *The Cardinal bird."*
>
> —W. S. Gallagher.

A canada goose in flight

Geese

TEACHER'S STORY

TO be called a goose should be considered most complimentary, for of all the birds the goose is probably the most intelligent. An observant lady who keeps geese on her farm assures me that no animal, not even dog or horse, has the intelligence of the goose. She says that these birds learn a lesson after a few repetitions, and surely her geese were patterns of obedience. While I was watching them one morning, they started for the brook via the corn field; she called to them sharply, "No, no, you mustn't go that way!" They stopped and conferred; she spoke again and they waited, looking at her as if to make up their minds to this exercise of self-sacrifice; but when she spoke the third time they left the corn field and took the other path to the brook. She could bring her geese into their house at any time of day by calling to them, "Home, home!" As soon as they heard these words, they would start and not stop until the last one was housed.

In ancient Greece maidens made pets of geese; and often there was such a devotion between the bird and girl that when the latter died her statue with that of the goose was carved on her burial tablet. The loyalty of a pet goose came under the observation of Miss Ada Georgia. A lone gander was the special pet of a small boy in Elmira, N. Y., who took sole care of him. The bird obeyed commands like a dog but would never let his little master out of his sight if he could avoid it; occasionally he would appear in the school yard, where the pupils would tease him by pretending to attack his master at the risk of being whipped with his wings so severely that it was a test of bravery among the boys to so challenge him. His fidelity to his master was extreme; once when the boy was ill in bed, the bird wandered about the yard honking disconsolately and refused to eat; he was driven to the side of the house where his master could look from the window and he immediately cheered up, took his food and refused to leave his post beneath the window while the illness lasted.

The goose is a stately bird whether on land or water; its long legs give it good proportions when walking, and the neck, being so much longer than that of the duck, gives an appearance of grace and dignity. The duck on the other hand is beautiful only when on the water or on the wing; its short legs, placed far back and far out at the sides, make it a most ungraceful walker. The beak of the goose is harder in texture and is not flat like the duck's; no wonder the bird was a favorite with the ancient Greeks, for the high ridge from the beak to the forehead resembles much the famous Grecian nose. The plumage of geese is very beautiful and abundant and for this reason they are profitable domestic birds. The "picking" occurs late in summer when the feathers are nearly ready to be molted; at this time the geese flap their wings often and set showers of loose feathers flying. A stocking or a bag is slipped over the bird's head and she is turned breast side up, with her head firmly between the knees or under the arm of the picker. The tips of the feathers are seized with the fingers and come out easily; only the breast, the under parts and the feathers beneath the wings are plucked. Geese do not seem to suffer while being plucked except through the temporary inconvenience and ignominy of having their heads thrust into a bag; it hurts their dignity more than their bodies.

The wings of geese are very large and beautiful; although our domestic geese have lost their powers of flight to a great extent, yet they often stretch their wings and take little flying hops, teetering along as if they can scarcely keep to earth; this must surely be reminiscent of the old instinct for traveling in the skies. The tail of the goose is a half

A pair of canada geese and two goslings

circle and is spread when flying; although it is short, it seems to be sufficiently long to act as a rudder. The legs of the goose are much longer than those of the duck; they are not set so far back toward the rear of the body, and, therefore, the goose is the much better runner of the two. The track made by the goose's foot is a triangle with two scallops on one side made by the webs between the three front toes; the hind toe is placed high up; the foot and the unfeathered portion of the leg, protected by scales, are used as oars when the bird is swimming. When she swims forward rapidly, her feet extend out behind her and act on the principle of a propeller; but when swimming around in the pond she uses them at almost right angles to the body. Although they are such excellent oars they are also efficient on land; although when running, her body may waddle somewhat, her head and neck are held aloft in stately dignity.

The Toulouse are our common gray geese; the Embdens are pure white with orange bill and bright blue eyes. The African geese have a black head with a large black knob on the base of the black bill; the neck is long, snakelike, light gray, with a dark stripe down the back; the wings and tail are dark gray; there is a dewlap at the throat. The brown Chinese geese have also a black beak and a black knob at the base of the bill. The neck is light brown with a dull yellowish stripe down the neck. The back is dark brown, breast, wings and tail grayish

These lesser Canada geese are joined by several white-fronted geese and a lone snow goose. It is not uncommon to see several species of geese traveling together in a flock when migrating

brown. The white Chinese are shaped like the brown Chinese but the knob and bill are orange and the eyes light blue.

The Habits of Geese

Geese are monogamous and are loyal to their mates. Old-fashioned people declare that they choose their mates on Saint Valentine's Day, but this is probably a pretty myth; when once mated, the pair live together year after year until one dies; an interesting instance of this is one of the traditions in my own family. A fine pair of geese belonging to my pioneer grandfather had been mated for several years and had reared handsome families; but one spring a conceited young gander fell in love with the old goose, and, as he was young and lusty, he whipped her legitimate lord and master and triumphantly carried her away, although she was manifestly disgusted with this change in her domestic fortunes. The old gander sulked and refused to be comforted by the blandishments of any young goose whatever. Later the old pair disappeared from the farmyard and the upstart gander was left wifeless. It was inferred that the old couple had run away with each other into the encompassing wilderness and much sympathy was felt for them because of this sacrifice of their lives for loyalty. However, this was misplaced sentiment, for later in the summer the happy pair was discovered in a distant "slashing" with a fine family of goslings and were all brought home in triumph. The old gander, while not able to cope with his rival, was still able to trounce any of the animal marauders which approached his home and family.

The goose lines her nest with down and the soft feathers which she plucks from her breast. The gander is very devoted to his goose while she is sitting; he talks to her in gentle tones and is fierce in her defence. The eggs are about twice as large as those of the hen and have the ends more rounded. The period of incubation is four weeks. The goslings are beautiful little creatures, covered with soft down, and have large, bright eyes. The parents give them most careful attention from the first. One family which I studied consisted of the parents and eighteen goslings. The mother was a splendid African bird; she walked with dignified step, her graceful neck assuming serpentine curves; and she always carried her beak "lifted," which gave her an appearance of majestic haughtiness. The father was just a plebeian white gander, probably of Embden descent, but he was a most efficient protector. The family always formed a procession in going to the creek, the majestic mother at the head, the goslings following her and the gander bringing up the rear to be sure there were no stragglers; if a gosling strayed away or fell behind, the male went after it, pushing it back into the family circle. When entering the coop at night he pushed the little ones in gently with his bill; when the goslings took their first swim both parents gently pushed them into the water, "rooted them in," as the farmer said. Any attempt to take liberties with the brood was met with bristling anger and defiance on the part of the gander; the mistress of the farm told me that he had whipped her black and blue when she tried to interfere with the goslings.

The gander and goose always show suspicion and resentment by opening the mouth wide, making a hissing noise, showing the whole round tongue in mocking defiance. When the gander attacks, he thrusts his head forward, even with or below the level of his back, and seizes his victim firmly with his hard, toothed bill so that it cannot get away, and then with his strong wings beats the life out of it. I remember vividly a whipping which a gander gave me when I was a child, holding me fast by the blouse while he laid on the blows.

Geese feed much more largely upon land vegetation than do ducks; a good growth of clover and grass make excellent pasture for them; in the water, they feed upon water plants but do not eat insects and animals to any extent.

Undoubtedly goose language is varied and expresses many things. Geese talk to each other and call from afar; they shriek in warning and in general make such a turmoil that people do not enjoy it. The goslings, even when almost grown, keep up a constant "pee wee, pee wee," which is nerve-racking. There is a good opportunity for some interesting investigations in studying out just what the different notes of the geese mean.

The goose is very particular about her toilet; she cleans her breast and back and beneath her wings with her bill; and she cleans her bill with her foot; she also cleans the top of her head with her foot and the under side of her wing with the foot of that side. When oiling her feathers, she starts the oil gland flowing with her beak, then rubs her head over the gland until it is well oiled; she then uses her head as a "dauber" to apply the oil to the feathers of her back and breast. When thus polishing her feathers, she twists the head over and over and back and forth to add to its efficiency.

WILD GEESE

THERE is a sound, that, to the weather-wise farmer, means cold and snow, even though it is heard through the hazy atmosphere of an Indian summer day; and that is the honking of wild geese as they pass on their southward journey. And there is not a more interesting sight anywhere in the autumn landscape than the wedge-shaped flock of these long-necked birds with their leader at the front apex. "The wild goose trails his harrow," sings the poet; but only the aged can remember the old-fashioned harrow which makes this simile graphic. The honking which reveals to us the passing flock, before our eyes can discern the birds against the sky, is the call of the wise old gander who is the leader, to those following him, and their return salute. He knows the way on this long thousand-mile journey, and knows it by the to-pography of the country. If ever fog or storm hides the earth from his view, he is likely to become confused, to the dismay of his flock, which follows him to the earth with many lonely and distressful cries.

The northern migration takes place in April and May, and the southern from October to December. The journey is made with stops for rest and refreshment at certain selected places, usually some se-cluded pond or lake. The food of wild geese consists of water plants, seeds and corn, and some of the smaller animals living in water. Al-though the geese come to rest on the water, they go to the shore to feed. In California, the wild geese are dreaded visitors of the corn-fields, and men with guns are employed regularly to keep them off.

The nests are made of sticks lined with down, usually along the shores of streams, sometimes on tree stumps and sometimes in de-serted nests of the osprey. There are only four or five eggs laid and both parents are devoted to the young, the gander bravely defending his nest and family from the attacks of any enemies.

Although there are several species of wild geese on the Atlantic Coast, the one called by this name is usually the Canada goose. This bird is a superb creature, brown above and gray beneath, with head, neck, tail, bill and feet of black. These black trimmings are highly orna-mental and, as if to emphasize them, there is a white crescent-shaped "bib" extending from just back of the eyes underneath the head. This white patch is very striking, and gives one the impression of a ban-dage for sore throat. It is regarded as a call-color, and is supposed to help keep the flock together; the side tail-coverts are also white and make another guide to follow.

Often some wounded or wearied bird of the migrating flock spends the winter in farmyards with domestic geese. One morning a neighbor of mine found that during the night a wild gander, injured in some way, had joined his flock. The stranger was treated with much courtesy by its new companions as well as by the farmer's family and soon seemed perfectly at home. The next spring he mated with one of the domestic geese. In the late summer, my neighbor, mindful of wild geese habits, clipped the wings of the gander so that he would be unable to join any passing flock of his wild relatives. As the mi-

Canada geese flying in formation

grating season approached, the gander became very uneasy; not only was he uneasy and unhappy always but he insisted that his wife share his misery of unrest. He spent days in earnest remonstrance with her and, lifting himself by his cropped wings to the top of the barnyard fence, he insisted that she keep him company on this, for web feet, uneasy resting place. Finally, after many days of tribulation, the two valiantly started south on foot. News was received of their progress for some distance and then they were lost to us. During the winter our neighbor visited a friend living eighteen miles to the southward and found in his barnyard the errant pair. They had become tired of migrating by tramping and had joined the farmer's flock; but we were never able to determine the length of time required for this journey.

LESSON

Leading thought— Geese are the most intelligent of the domesticated birds, and they have many interesting habits.

Method— This lesson should not be given unless there are geese where the pupils may observe them. The questions should be given a few at a time and answered individually by the pupils after the observations are made.

Observations—

1. What is the chief difference between the appearance of a goose

and a duck? How does the beak of the goose differ from that of the duck in shape and in texture? Describe the nostrils and their situation.

2. What is the difference in shape between the neck of the goose and that of the duck?

3. What can you say about the plumage of geese? How are geese "picked?" At what time of year? From what parts of the body are the feathers plucked?

4. Are the wings of the goose large compared with the body? How do geese exercise their wings? Describe the tail of the goose and how it is used.

5. How do the legs and feet of the goose differ from those of the duck? Describe the goose's foot. How many toes are webbed? Where is the other toe? What is the shape of the track made by the goose's foot? Which portions of the legs are used for oars? When the goose is swimming forward where are her feet? When turning around how does she use them? Does the goose waddle when walking or running as a duck does? Why? Does a goose toe-in when walking? Why?

6. Describe the shape and color of the following breeds of domestic geese: The Toulouse, the Embden, the African, and Chinese.

HABITS OF GEESE

1. What is the chief food of geese? What do they find in the water to eat? How does their food differ from that of ducks?

2. How do geese differ from hens in the matter of mating and nesting? At what time of year do geese mate? Does a pair usually remain mated for life?

3. Describe the nest and compare the eggs with those of hens. Describe the young goslings in general appearance. With what are they covered? What care do the parents give to their goslings? Describe how the parents take their family afield. How do they induce their goslings to go into the water for the first time? How do they protect them from enemies?

4. How does the gander or goose fight? What are the chief weapons? How is the head held when the attack is made?

5. How does the goose clean her feathers, wings and feet? How

does she oil her feathers? Where does she get the oil and with what does she apply it?

6. How much of goose language do you understand? What is the note of alarm? How is defiance and distrust expressed? How does a goose look when hissing? What is the constant note of the gosling?

7. Give such instances as you may know illustrating the intelligence of geese, their loyalty and bravery.

8. Write an English Theme on "The Canada Goose, its appearance, nesting habits, and migrations."

Supplementary reading— Birds that Hunt and are Hunted, Blanchan; "In Quest of Waptonk The Wild," *Northern Trails*, Long; "The Homesickness of Kehonka," *Kindred of the Wild*, Roberts; *Wild Geese*, Celia Thaxter.

The Turkey

THAT the turkey and not the eagle should have been chosen for our national bird, was the conviction of Benjamin Franklin. It is a native of our country, it is beautiful as to plumage, and like the American Indian, it has never yielded entirely to the influences of civilization. Through the hundreds of years of domestication it still retains many of its wild habits. In fact, it has many qualities in common with the red man. Take for instance its sun dance, which any one can witness who is willing to get up early enough in the morning and who has a flock of turkeys at hand. Miss Ada Georgia made a pilgrimage to witness this dance and she describes it thus: "While the dawn was still faint and gray, the long row of birds on the ridge-pole stood up, stretched legs and wings and flew down into the orchard beside the barnyard and began a curious, high-stepping, 'flip-flop' dance on the frosty grass. It consisted of little, awkward, up-and-down jumps, varied by forward springs of about a foot, with lifted wings. Both hens and males danced, the latter alternately strutting and hopping and all 'singing,' the hens calling 'Quit, quit,' the males accompanying with a high-keyed rattle,

A turkey poult

sounding like a hard wood stick drawn rapidly along a picket fence. As the sun came up and the sky brightened, the exhibition ended suddenly when 'The Captain,' a great thirty pound gobbler and leader of the flock, made a rush at one of his younger brethren who had dared to be spreading a tail too near to his majesty."

The bronze breed resembles most closely our native wild turkey and is therefore chosen for this lesson. The colors and markings of the plumage form the bronze turkey's chief beauty. From the skin of the neck, reaching half way to the middle of the back is a collar of glittering bronze with greenish and purple iridescence, each feather tipped with a narrow jet band. The remainder of the back is black except that each feather is edged with bronze. The breast is like the collar and at its center is a tassel of black bristles called the beard, which hangs limply downward when the birds are feeding; but when the gobbler stiffens his muscles to strut, this beard is thrust proudly forth. Occasionally the hen turkeys have a beard. The long quills, or primaries, of the wings are barred across with bands of black and white; the secondaries are very dark, luminous brown, with narrower bars of white. Each feather of the fan-shaped tail is banded with black and brown and ends with a black bar tipped with white; the tail coverts are lighter brown but also have the black margin edged with white. The colors of the hen are like those of the gobbler except that the bronze brilliance of breast, neck and wings is dimmed by the faint line of white which tips each feather.

The heads of all are covered with a warty wrinkled skin, bluish white on the crown, grayish blue about the eyes, and the other parts red. Beneath the throat is a hanging fold called the wattle, and above the beak a fleshy pointed knob called the caruncle, which on the gobbler is prolonged so that it hangs over and below the beak. When the bird is angry these carunculated parts swell and grow more vivid in color, seeming to be gorged with blood. The color of the skin about the head is more extensive and brilliant in the gobblers than in the hens. The beak is slightly curved, short, stout, and sharp-pointed, yellowish at the tip and dark at the base.

The eyes are bright, dark hazel with a thin red line of iris. Just back of the eye is the ear, seemingly a mere hole, and yet it leads to a very efficient ear, upon which every smallest sound impinges.

The legs of the young turkeys are nearly black, fading to a brownish gray when mature. The legs and feet are large and stout, the middle toe of the three front ones being nearly twice the length of the one on either side; the hind toe is the shortest of the four. On the inner side of the gobbler's legs, about one-third the bare space above the foot, is a wicked looking spur which is a most effective weapon. The wings are large and powerful; the turkey flies well for such a large bird and usually roosts high, choosing trees or the ridge-pole of the barn for this purpose.

In many ways the turkeys are not more than half domesticated. They insistently prefer to spend their nights out of doors instead of under a roof. They are also great wanderers and thrive best when allowed to forage in the fields and woods for a part of their food.

The gobbler is the most vainglorious bird known to us; when he struts to show his flock of admiring hens how beautiful he is, he lowers his wings and spreads the stiff primary quills until their tips scrape the ground, lifting meanwhile into a semi-circular fan his beautiful tail feathers; he protrudes his chest, raises the iridescent plumage of his neck like a ruff to make a background against which he throws back his red, white and blue decorated head. He moves forward with slow and mincing steps and calls attention to his grandeur by a series of most aggressive "gobbles." But we must say for the gobbler that, although he is vain, he is also a brave fighter. When beginning a fight he advances with wings lowered and sidewise as if guarding his body with the spread wing. The neck and the sharp beak are outstretched and he makes the attack so suddenly, that it is impossible to see whether he strikes with both wing and beak or only with the latter, as with fury he pounces upon his adversary, apparently striving to rip his neck open with his spurs.

Turkey hens usually begin to lay in April in this latitude and much earlier in more southern states. At nesting time each turkey hen strays off alone, seeking the most secluded spot she can find to lay the large, oval, brown-speckled eggs. Silent and sly, she slips away to the place daily, by the most round-about ways, and never moving in the direction of the nest when she thinks herself observed. Sometimes the sight of any person near her nest will cause her to desert it. The writer has spent many hours when a child, sneaking in fence corners and behind stumps and tree trunks, stalking turkeys' nests. Incubation takes four weeks. The female is a most persistent sitter and care should be taken to see that she gets a good supply of food and water at this time. Good sound corn or wheat is the best food for her at this period. When sitting she is very cross and will fight most courageously when molested on her nest.

Turkey nestlings are rather large, with long, bare legs and scrawny thin necks, and they are very delicate during the first six weeks of their lives. Their call is a plaintive "peep, weep," and when a little turkey feels lost its cry is expressive of great fear and misery. But if the mother is freely ranging, she does not seem to be much affected by the needs of her brood; she will fight savagely for them if they are near her, but if they stray, and they usually do, she does not seem to miss or hunt for them, but strides serenely on her way, keeping up a constant crooning "kr-rit, kr-rit," to encourage them to follow. As a consequence, the

A pair of wild turkey cross the road

chicks are lost or get draggled and chilled by struggling through wet grass and leaves, that are no obstacle to the mother's strong legs, and thus many die. If the mother is confined in a coop it should be so large and roomy that she can move about without trampling on the chicks, and it should have a dry floor, since dampness is fatal to the little ones.

For the first week the chicks should be fed five times a day, and for the next five weeks they should have three meals a day. They should be given only just about enough to fill each little crop and none left over to be trodden under their awkward little feet. Their quarters should be kept clean and free from vermin.

LESSON

Leading thought— The turkey is a native of America. It was introduced into Spain from Mexico in about 1518, and since then has been domesticated. However, there are still in some parts of the country flocks of wild turkeys. It is a beautiful bird and has interesting habits.

Method—If the pupils could visit a flock of turkeys the lesson would be given to a better advantage. If this is impossible, ask the questions a few at a time and let those pupils who have opportunities for observing the turkeys give their answers before the class.

Observations—

1. Of what breed are the turkeys you are studying, Bronze, Black, Buff, White Holland or Narragansett?

2. What is the general shape and size of the turkey? Describe its plumage, noting every color which you can see in it. Does the plumage of the hen turkey differ from that of the gobbler?

3. What is the covering of the head of the turkey, what is its color and how far does it extend down the neck of the bird? Is it always the same color, and if not, what causes the change? Is the head covering alike in shape and size on the male and the female? What is the part called that hangs from the front of the throat below the beak? From above the beak?

4. What is the color of the beak? Is it short or long, straight or curved? Where are the nostrils situated?

5. What is the color of the turkey's eyes? Do you think it is a keen-sighted bird?

6. Where are the ears? Do they show as plainly as a chicken's ears do? Are turkeys quick of hearing?

7. Do turkeys scratch like hens? Are they good runners? Describe the feet and legs as to shape, size and color. Has the male a spur on his legs, and if so, where is it situated? For what is it used?

8. Can turkeys fly well? Are the wings small or comparatively large and strong for the weight of the body? Do turkeys prefer high or low places for perching when they sleep? Is it well to house and confine them in small buildings and parks as is done with other fowls?

9. Tell, as nearly as you can discover by close observation, how the gobbler sets each part of his plumage when he is "showing off" or strutting. What do you think is the bird's purpose in thus exhibiting his fine feathers? Does the "King of the flock" permit any such action by other "gobblers" in his company?

10. Are turkeys timid and cowardly or independent and brave, ready to meet and fight anything which they think is threatening to their comfort and safety?

A group of turkeys is called a 'gang' or a 'rafter'

11. When turkeys fight, what parts of their bodies seem to be used as weapons? Does the male "gobble" during a fight, or only as a challenge or in triumph when victorious? Do the hen turkeys ever fight, or only the males?

12. How early in the spring does the turkey hen begin to lay? Does she nest about the poultry yard and the barns or is she likely to seek some secret and distant spot where she may hide her eggs? Describe the turkey's egg, as well as you can, as to color, shape and size. Can one tell it by the taste from an ordinary hen's egg? About how many eggs does the turkey hen lay in her nest before she begins to "get broody" and want to sit?

13. How many days of incubation are required to hatch the turkey chick? Is it as downy and pretty as other little chicks? How often should the young chicks be fed, and what food do you think is best for them? Are turkey chicks as hardy as other chicks?

14. Is the turkey hen generally a good mother? Is she cross or gentle when sitting and when brooding her young? Is it possible to keep the mother turkey as closely confined with her brood as it is with the mother hen? What supplies should be given to her in the way of food, grits, dust-baths, etc.?

Supplementary reading— Birds that Hunt and are Hunted, Blanchan.

LESSON

There are very good reasons for not studying birds' nests in summer, since too much familiarity on the part of eager children is something the birds do not understand and are likely, in consequence, to abandon both nest and locality. But after the birds have gone to sunnier climes and the empty nests are the only mementos we have of them, then we may study these habitations carefully and learn how to properly appreciate the small architects which made them. I think that every one of us who carefully examines the way that a nest is made must have a feeling of respect for its clever little builder.

I know of certain schools where the children make large collections of these winter nests, properly labelling each, and thus gaining a new interest in the bird life of their locality. A nest when collected should be labelled in the following manner:

Name of the bird which built the nest.

Where the nest was found.

If in a tree, what kind?

How high from the ground?

Bird Homes, by A. R. Dugmore, is a book which affords practical help in determining the species of birds which made the nests.

After a collection of nests has been made, let the pupils study them according to the following outline:

1. Where was the nest found?

    a. If on the ground, describe the locality.

    b. If on a plant, tree or shrub, tell the species, if possible.

    c. If on a tree, tell where it was on a branch, in a fork, or hanging by the end of the twigs.

    d. How high from the ground, and what was the locality?

    e. If on or in a building, how situated?

2. Did the nest have any arrangement to protect it from rain?

3. Give the size of the nest, the diameter of the inside and the outside; also the depth of the inside.

4. What is the form of the nest? Are its sides flaring or straight? Is the nest shaped like a cup, basket or pocket?

5. What materials compose the outside of the nest and how are they arranged?

A turkey nest in the woods

6. Of what materials is the lining made, and how are they arranged? If hair or feathers are used, on what creature did they grow?

7. How are the materials of the nest held together, that is, are they woven, plastered, or held in place by environment?

8. Had the nest anything peculiar about it either in situation, construction or material that would tend to render it invisible to the casual glance?